# PERSPECTIVES IN COGNITIVE NEUROSCIENCE

D1565226

Stephen M. Kosslyn

SERIES EDITOR

# MIND TIME

The Temporal Factor

in Consciousness

# Benjamin Libet

**HARVARD UNIVERSITY PRESS**
Cambridge, Massachusetts
London, England

First Harvard University Press paperback edition, 2005.

Library of Congress Cataloging-in-Publication Data

Libet, Benjamin, 1916–
Mind time : the temporal factor in consciousness / Benjamin Libet.
p.   cm.—(Perspectives in cognitive neuroscience)
Includes bibliographical references and index.
ISBN 0-674-01320-4 (cloth)
ISBN 0-674-01846-X (paper)
1. Consciousness.   2. Time perception.   3. Memory.   4. Cognitive neuroscience.
I. Title.   II. Series.
QP411.L538 2004
153—dc22        2003056934

*To Ralph Waldo Gerard, Sir John Eccles, and K. Allan C. Elliott*

# CONTENTS

Foreword    ix

Preface    xvii

1. Introduction to the Question    1

2. The Delay in Our Conscious Sensory Awareness    33

3. Unconscious and Conscious Mental Functions    90

4. Intention to Act: Do We Have Free Will?    123

5. Conscious Mental Field Theory: Explaining How the Mental Arises from the Physical    157

6. What Does It All Mean?    185

Bibliography    225

Index    241

# FOREWORD

I just typed the word "consciousness" into the search engine in Amazon.com, and it returned 2,670 titles. If I wait a few weeks, there will probably be more. Does the world really need another book on consciousness? Yes—if we are talking about the one you are holding in your hands, right now. This book is strikingly different from most of the others in one key respect: It focuses on empirical discoveries, not speculation or argument. Benjamin Libet has an enviable track record of producing solid empirical findings about the relationship between neural events and consciousness. And these findings are not simply reliable— they are also surprising. His discoveries were at first controversial, but have withstood the test of time. Surprising findings play a special role in science, given that they (by definition) upset the apple cart of conventional wisdom. His results must now be explained by any theory of consciousness and its neural underpinnings. This book gathers together Libet's contributions in one place, and puts them in context.

Libet's work has focused on temporal relations between neural events and experience. He is famous in part for discovering that we unconsciously decide to act well before we think we've made the decision to act. This finding has major implications for one of the deepest problems in philosophy and psychology, namely the problem of "free will."

First, a brief overview of the basic discovery: Libet asked people to move their wrist at a time of their choosing. The participants were asked to look at a moving dot that indicated the time, and note the precise time when they decided to flex their wrist. The participants reported having the intention about 200 milliseconds before they actually began to move. Libet also measured the "readiness potential" in the brain, which is revealed by activity recorded from the supplementary motor area of the brain (which is involved in controlling movements). This readiness potential occurred some 550 milliseconds before the action began. The brain events that produced the movement thus occurred about 350 milliseconds before the participant was aware of having made a decision. Libet shows that this disparity is not simply due to extra time required to note and report the time.

Why is this finding important? Consider two reasons: First, on the face of things, the finding suggests that being conscious of having made a decision might be best thought of as a *result* of brain processes that actually do the work, rather than as part of the causal chain of events leading up to a decision. Second, Libet points out that even if a movement were initiated by unconscious forces, there is nevertheless ample time to *veto* an act, once one is aware of one's intentions. Libet believes that this observation keeps the door open for traditional notions of "free will."

But does it? Consider an argument against free will, based on one developed in detail by Strawson (1994; see also *www.ucl.ac.uk/~uctytho/dfwVariousStrawsonG.html*):

1. At birth, one's thoughts, feelings and behavior are determined by genes, prenatal learning, and environmental stimuli.

2. Subsequent thoughts, feelings and behavior are built on the foundation present at birth—they are determined by one's genes, learning history, and present stimuli. All decisions and choices are based on reasons, and those reasons are a direct result of one's accumulation of experience, as modulated by genetic factors.

3. If one tries to change oneself, both the goals and methods of such change are themselves determined by genes, previous learning, and current environmental stimuli. What one *can* be is determined by what one already is.

4. Adding random factors would not confer free will. Klein (2002; Stapp, 2001; and others) notes that simply adding indeterminacy to a system does not make its actions free if they are not already free. In fact, adding randomness decreases freedom rather than increasing it. "Random behavior" is not "free will."

5. Thus, this argument goes, there's no free will to be exercised during the interval between when one becomes aware of an impending action and one performs it. Whether or not you will squelch the action is as determined as are the factors that initiate the action in the first place. Even if one has time to override one's unconscious urges, there's no free will at work if one's conscious decisions are themselves determined (cf. Wegner, 2002). Libet's "time to veto" no more confers the opportunity to exercise of free will than the time between putting eggs on the skittle and waiting for them to fry provides the eggs with the opportunity not to cook.

Nevertheless, at least to my mind, something smells right about Libet's proposal. In particular, the opposite of being "determined" is not necessarily being "random." Klein (2002) notes that classical deterministic views are rooted in a world view that is not in fact correct. Many events in the real world are not like pool balls, hitting one another and careening off the sides of the table in predictable ways. We know that many physical systems have chaotic elements: The way they respond to a perturbation depends on tiny—in principle, never precisely measurable—differences in their start state. Freeman (2000) and others have shown that at least some aspects of brain function are best conceived as such systems. Is it possible that the very nature of the brain confers free will? Kane (1996) has suggested as much, and I will summarize a version of the type of view he advocates (although he focuses on process that may occur when one is faced with difficult decisions, the basic ideas can be extended further).

Let's consider one possible way in which this feature of the brain may keep the door open for Libet's idea.

1. Libet is right to focus on consciousness when theorizing about free will: In order to employ free will, one must evaluate information in working memory. Such information includes the alternative choices, the rationales for each, and the anticipated consequences of making each choice (although not all this information must be in working memory at the same time). If an external force coerces us, or we are operating on "automatic pilot," we are not exercising free will.

2. The rationales and anticipated consequences—and even, depending on the situation, the alternative courses of action—are not simply "looked up" in memory, having been stashed away like notes in a file after previous encounters. Rather, one *con-*

*structs* rationales and anticipated consequences, as appropriate for the specific situation at hand. This construction process may rely in part on chaotic processes. Such processes are not entirely determined by one's learning history (even as filtered by one's genes). By analogy, consider the path of a raindrop dribbling down a pane of glass. It zigs, it zags, tracing a path best explained with the aid of chaotic principles. The same raindrop, striking precisely the same place on that pane on a warmer day (which would cause the glass to be in a slightly different state) would take a different path. In chaotic systems, very small differences in start state can produce large differences downstream. The pane of glass is like the state of the brain at any instant. Depending on what one was just thinking about, the brain is in a different "start state" (i.e., different information is partially activated, different associations are primed) when one constructs rationales and anticipated consequences—which will affect how one decides. (Note that this idea does not simply move the problem back a step: What one was just thinking itself was in part a result of nondeterministic processes.) Our thoughts, feelings and behavior are not determined; we can have novel insights as well as "second thoughts."

3. Given the choices, rationales, and anticipated consequences, one decides what do on the basis of "what one is" (mentally speaking, to use Strawson's term, which includes one's knowledge, goals, values, and beliefs). "What one is" consists in part of information in memory, which plays a key role in the processes that construct the alternatives, rationales, and anticipated consequences. In addition, "what one is" governs how one actually makes the decisions. And making that decision and experiencing the actual consequences in turn modifies "what one is," which then affects both how one constructs alternatives, ratio-

nales and anticipated consequences and how one makes decisions in the future. Thus, with time one's decisions construct what one is.

We are not simply accumulators of environmental events, filtered by our genetic make-ups. We bring something novel and unique to each situation—ourselves. Nietzsche (1886, as quoted in Strawson, 1994, p. 15) commented, "The *causa sui* is the best self-contradiction that has been conceived so far." Maybe not.

4. This brings us back to the implications of Libet's discovery, and suggests a way in which we can exercise free will during that crucial interval between when we become aware of that action and the action begins: The sum of "what one is" leads one to make a specific decision. Such a decision can occur unconsciously, and initiate an action. However, upon realizing that one is about to perform a specific act, one can consider its likely consequences and the rationales pro and con for performing that act; this information is constructed on the spot, and is not present during unconscious processing. And, based on "what one is," one then can decide not to move ahead—or, if the action has begun, one can decide to squelch it (and thus one is not limited to the 200 milliseconds Libet has measured). As Libet notes, we can in fact veto an action, and that decision is not a foregone conclusion. We make decisions for reasons, and those reasons are *our* reasons.

Libet has made a fundamental discovery. If the timing of mental events is as he describes, then we not only have "free will" in principle—but we also have the opportunity to exercise that free will.

The ideas I've briefly sketched are variants of many others (cf. Kane, 1996), and address issues that have been discussed (sometimes heatedly) for thousands of years. I've not mentioned the issue of "ultimate responsibility"—whether one is completely responsible for "what one is." Given that one cannot control the genetic cards one's parents dealt one, the sense of "free will" developed here seems to go only so far. However, Libet's veto idea leads us to take a step back, and reframe the question: Instead of asking whether one is "ultimately responsible" for every aspect of what one is, why not ask whether one is "proximally responsible" for the *effects* of every aspect of what one is on what one does? Can we choose—based on what we've chosen to become—to override some impulses and express others?

I hope these brief reflections have conveyed two essential points. The first is that these are extraordinarily knotty issues, and the question of the role of consciousness in free will is not likely to be resolved soon. And the second is that we are entering a new era in discussing such questions. No longer are we restricted to the arm chair and the silver tongue. We now have objective data. This book makes a crucial contribution in providing grist for the mill of anyone interested in consciousness, free will, responsibility, or the relation of mind and body.

I hope you enjoy reading this book as much as I did.

S. M. Kosslyn

## References

Freeman, W. J. 2000. Brain dynamics: Brain chaos and intentionality. In *Integrative Neuroscience. Bringing Together Biological, Psychological, and Clinical Models of the Human Brain*, ed. E. Gordon. Sydney, Australia: Harwood Academic Publishers, pp. 163–171.

Kane, R. 1996. *The Significance of Free Will*. New York: Oxford University Press.

Klein, S. 2002. Libet's research on the timing of conscious intention to act: A commentary. *Consciousness and Cognition* 11:273–279.

Stapp, H. P. 2001. Quantum theory and the role of the mind in nature. *Foundations of Physics* 31: 1465–1499.

Strawson, G. 1994. The impossibility of moral responsibility. *Philosophical Studies* 75: 5–24.

Wegner, D. M. 2002. *The Illusion of Conscious Will*. Cambridge, Mass.: MIT Press.

# PREFACE

How did I come to write this book?

We had made some surprising discoveries of how the brain is involved in the production of conscious subjective experience and of unconscious mental functions. Where and how conscious experience arises, and how that differs from unconscious mental activities, are questions of profound interest not only to me but also to many others. Our discoveries were arrived at experimentally. They were based not on speculative theorizing but on factual findings. This is in contrast to most writings and proposals by philosophers and by some neuroscientists, physicists, and others on these subjects.

I thought, therefore, that our discoveries and the many important implications that they generate should be made available to a wide general audience as well as to philosophers, scientists, and clinicians who deal with mental problems. An especially important feature of this presentation is the demonstration that mind-brain problems and cerebral bases for conscious experience can be studied experimentally.

How did all this happen? You must recognize that conscious experience can be studied only in awake human subjects who can give you a report of their experience. Non-human animals may very well have conscious experiences, but there is no good way of studying those experiences validly. I was given the unique opportunity to study human subjects who were undergoing neurosurgical therapy from Dr. Bertram Feinstein. Bert and I were formerly colleagues in the Biomechanics Lab at UCSF, where he was a neurologist. After three years of training in neurosurgery in Sweden, Bert started a practice at the Mt. Zion Hospital in San Francisco. He also wanted to use the opportunities of access to the human brain to conduct significant risk-free investigations, and he offered me the opportunity to conduct such studies. The therapy required the placement of electrodes at specified structures within the brain. I jumped at the chance of studying the electrical activity of cerebral nerve cells and electrical stimulation of appropriate nerve cells, in relation to reports of conscious experiences by patients. I should emphasize that our experimental procedures added no risk to the patients. They were done with the informed consent of the patients and not one of our activities produced any difficulties or damage. The patients were in fact remarkably cooperative with our studies.

Dr. Feinstein was himself easygoing and cooperative in the operating room. He let me design the experiments, and he did not display an autocratic prima donna attitude during surgery. After almost twenty years of this collaboration, Feinstein died prematurely in 1978. Following his untimely death, my lab turned to the study of voluntary action, in which we could use normal subjects. We also carried out a fundamentally important study on the unique difference between detection of a sensory signal and the development of conscious awareness of that signal (Libet et al., 1991). For this latter study, we had available patients with permanently implanted stimulating electrodes, in a sensory pathway in the brain, for the relief of intractable pain. These patients were made available to us by the cooperation of Dr. Y. Hosobuchi and Dr. N. M. Barbaro, neurosurgeons at UCSF. That work was also made possible by Michael Merzenich, Professor of Physiology, who generously provided a suitable space and computer equipment for our use at UCSF.

All these studies began in 1959, with the added collaboration of W. Watson Alberts as a biophysicist, and Elwood ("Bob") W. Wright, a biomedical engineer. Watson left the group in 1971 to become a successful administrator at the National Institute of Nervous and Mental Diseases. He was replaced by Curtis Gleason, a bioelectric engineer. I owe much of our effectiveness to the contributions of this team of collaborators. I must also express our appreciation to the many patients who cooperated in the studies. In addition, a group of ten graduate students in psychology were enthusiastic subjects in our experimental studies of voluntary action and conscious intention to act.

The three neuroscientists to whom I am dedicating this book were the chief mentors in my scientific career. Ralph Waldo Gerard, starting with my graduate work at the University of Chicago, introduced me to imaginative research in neuroscience and maintained his faith in my abilities even during my low period. Sir John Eccles brought me into modern experimental neuroscience (during a year-long period of research collaboration at the Australian National University) and supported my working on mind-brain relationships, even when that work was not popular among neuroscientists. K. Allan C. Elliott provided an example of rigor in the design and reporting of experimental work during a three-year collaboration on neurochemistry of the brain at the Institute of the Pennsylvania Hospital in Philadelphia.

I am grateful to my grandson Victor Libet and my daughters Gayla and Moreen Libet, for their helpful comments as lay readers of early versions of the manuscript. I also thank my friends Robert Doty and Anders Lundberg for their valuable advice and continuous encouragement and support. Comments by Michael Fisher, science editor for the Harvard University Press, led to a major reorganization of the coverage in the book. Elizabeth Collins provided skilled editing. I am grateful to Stephen Kosslyn for his excellent and meaningful Foreword.

Finally, I benefited from my wife Fay, my children (Julian, Moreen, Ralph, and Gayla), and my grandchildren (Victor, Anna, Leah, Lev, and Stavit).

# MIND TIME

# 1

## INTRODUCTION TO THE QUESTION

> Something happens when to a certain brain state a
> certain "consciousness" corresponds. A genuine glimpse
> into what it is would be *the* scientific achievement before
> which all past achievements would pale.
>
> —William James (1899)

You stop to admire the intense blue of a flower; you feel happy
with the antics of a young child; you feel pain in an arthritic
shoulder; you listen to the majestic music of Handel's *Messiah*
and feel moved by its majesty; you feel sad about a friend's ill-
ness; you feel you can make a free volitional choice of what
to do about a job and when to do it; you are aware of your
thoughts, beliefs, and inspirations; you are aware of your own
self as a real and reactive being.

All of these feelings and awarenesses are part of your subjective inner life. They are subjective in the sense that they are accessible *only* to the individual subject who is experiencing them.
They are *not* evident in and cannot be described by observations
of the physical brain.

Our subjective inner life is what really matters to us as human beings. Yet we know and understand little of how it arises and how it functions in our conscious will to act. We do know that the physical brain is essential to and intimately involved in the manifestations of our conscious, subjective experiences.

That fact gives rise to some fundamentally important questions.

### The Problem: Relating Brain Activities to Mental Functions

Appropriate nerve cell activities can certainly influence the content, or even the existence, of subjective experiences. Is the reverse true? That is, can our conscious intentions really influence or direct the nerve cell activities in the performance of a freely voluntary act?

Our subjective experiences are based on widespread networks of thousands of nerve cells, located in separate places in the brain. How is it possible for our experience, like a visual image, to appear subjectively in a unified form?

There is a further important issue when considering conscious experience. Many of our mental functions are carried out *unconsciously,* without conscious awareness. The considerable experimental and clinical evidence for that assertion is covered in later chapters. The role of unconscious mental processes in our emotional existence was, of course, prominently developed by Sigmund Freud and others. The question in the context of our present interest becomes, How does the brain distinguish between conscious and unconscious mental events?

Finally, there is the most mysterious of these questions: How can the *physical activities* of nerve cells in the brain give rise to the *nonphysical phenomena of conscious subjective experiences,* which include sensory awareness of the external world, thoughts, feelings of beauty, inspiration, spirituality, soulfulness, and so on? How can the gap between the "physical" (the brain) and the "mental" (our conscious, subjective experiences) be bridged?

There have been many proposed answers to these profound questions (for example, see Hook, 1960). These have come mainly from philosophical and religious sources, although contributions from neuroscientists have begun to appear in recent years. Religious proposals are clearly metaphysical beliefs, not scientifically testable. Those from philosophers have been largely theoretical speculative models that are mostly untestable.

As the philosopher of science Karl Popper (1992) pointed out, if a proposal or hypothesis cannot be tested in a way that could potentially falsify the proposal, then the proposer can offer any view without the possibility of its being contradicted. In that case, a proposal can offer any view without being disproved. Proposals that are untestable in that sense have been made not only by philosophers and theologians but even by some scientists. Many scientists like to think their own experimental research—for example, in immunology or motor control or theoretical physics and cosmology—provides a basis for informed speculations on the nature of conscious experience and the brain. Although often interesting, these speculations are mostly untestable. However, some of these proposals provide suggestive scientific approaches to the problems, and some of the philosophical analyses help to define the nature of the problems and some limitations on the kinds of answers one can hope to achieve.

It is not the intention of this book to present a full review of the literature in these areas. The goal of the book is to show that it is possible to deal experimentally with the problems in the relation between brain and conscious experience. Our own studies produced direct discoveries with fundamental implications, and these form the major coverage in the book. Our intracranial physiological observations were directly related to reports of conscious experiences by awake human subjects. That approach has been relatively unique in this field of interest. Related experimental studies and philosophical views are discussed, when relevant and desirable for facilitating the reader's understanding of our studies. (For a general history of discoveries in the human brain, see Marshall and Magoun, 1998.)

## General Views on Mind and Matter

At one pole is the determinist materialist position. In this philosophy, observable matter is the only reality and everything, including thought, will, and feeling, can be explained only in terms of matter and the natural laws that govern matter. The eminent scientist Francis Crick (codiscoverer of the genetic molecular code) states this view elegantly (Crick and Koch, 1998): "You, your joys and your sorrows, your memories and your ambitions, your sense of personal identity and free will, are in fact no more than the behavior of a vast assembly of nerve cells and their associated molecules. As Lewis Carroll's Alice might have phrased it: 'You're nothing but a pack of neurons (nerve cells).'" According to this determinist view, your awareness of yourself and the world around you is simply the by-product or epiphenomenon of neuronal activities, with no independent ability to affect or control neuronal activities.

Is this position a "proven" scientific theory? I shall state, straight out, that this determinist materialist view is a belief system; it is not a scientific theory that has been verified by direct tests. It is true that scientific discoveries have increasingly produced powerful evidence for the ways in which mental abilities, and even the nature of one's personality, are dependent on, and can be controlled by, specific structures and functions of the brain. However, the nonphysical nature of subjective awareness, including the feelings of spirituality, creativity, conscious will, and imagination, is not describable or explainable directly by the physical evidence alone.

As a neuroscientist investigating these issues for more than thirty years, I can say that these subjective phenomena are not predictable by knowledge of neuronal function. This is in contrast to my earlier views as a young scientist, when I believed in the validity of determinist materialism. That was before I began my research on brain processes in conscious experience, at age 40. There is no guarantee that the phenomenon of awareness and its concomitants will be explainable in terms of presently known physics.

In fact, conscious mental phenomena are not reducible to or explicable by knowledge of nerve cell activities. You could look into the brain and see nerve cell interconnections and neural messages popping about in immense profusion. But you would not observe any conscious mental subjective phenomena. Only a report by the individual who is experiencing such phenomena could tell you about them.

Francis Crick demonstrated his scientific credentials by terming his physicalist-determinist view an "astonishing *hypothesis*," awaiting future developments that might produce more adequate answers. But many scientists and philosophers appear not to realize that their rigid view that determinism is valid is still based on *faith*. They really don't have the answer.

Actually, even the nonmental physical world exhibits uncertainties (quantum theory) as well as chaotic behaviors that make a deterministic predictability of events impossible. At a small conference on these issues, the eminent theoretical physicist Eugene Wigner was asked whether physics could ever explain consciousness. Wigner replied, "Physics can't even explain physics," let alone consciousness! The more meaningful question, therefore, would be: Does the phenomenon of conscious experience, and its relation to the physical brain, fully obey the known rules and laws of the physical world? (More on this later.)

At the opposite pole from determinist materialism are beliefs that the mind is separable from the brain *(dualism)*. A religious version of dualism may maintain a belief in the existence of a soul that is somehow part of the body during life, but can separate and take off to variously defined destinations of immortality after death.

I shall state, at once, that the latter is absolutely tenable as a *belief*. The same is true for most other philosophical and religious proposals. There is nothing in all of scientific evidence that directly contradicts such beliefs. Indeed, they do not fall within the purview of scientific knowledge (see Karl Popper's position, described earlier).

A beautiful example of the scientific process was given by Einstein's proposal that light is subject to the same gravitational influences as matter. However, to demonstrate the gravitational effect on light requires that the light pass near an object of immense mass, one far greater than that available on earth. The difficulty in providing a proper test prevented full acceptance of

Einstein's proposal. Fortunately, around 1920 a complete solar eclipse occurred. The light from a star located on the other side of the sun passed near the sun on its way to earth and was visible during the eclipse. Indeed, the star's apparent position was altered, as the light was bent from its path by the "pull" of the sun. Had the light not been bent, Einstein's proposal would have been falsified (contradicted).

### Is There Any Scientific
### Approach to the Mind-Brain Problem?

Is there some way to arrive at convincing knowledge of how conscious subjective experience arises? Is there a way to do this that is based on observable evidence?

We must first recognize that the brain is the physical "organ" for conscious and unconscious mental functions. For life as we know it, the necessity of the appropriate function and structure of the brain is incontrovertible. There is no objective evidence for the existence of conscious phenomena apart from the brain. (A *belief* in a separable conscious soul is not excluded, as noted previously.) Perhaps the most convincing piece of evidence that it is the brain and not any other bodily structure that is crucial lies in the effects of a complete severing (transaction) of the spinal cord at its junction with the brain. This unfortunate event occurs not infrequently in accidents in which the neck is "broken," as in the recently publicized case of the actor Christopher Reeves. The patient remains the *same conscious person* he was before the accident. However, he loses all control of body movements from the neck down, including breathing movements, as well as all sensations that are carried by spinal nerves from the body to the brain. Interruption of the nerve pathways that connect the brain with the spinal cord is the reason for the loss of sensory and motor control below the neck. The person does remain aware of all the important sensations arising with intact nerve connections to the head. And, if the brain is functional, the person retains awareness of his thoughts, feelings, and self.

On the other hand, damage to the brain itself can result in the loss of various conscious functions, or even a permanent loss of consciousness, depending on the sites of the damage. It is the loss of brain function that truly defines the end of conscious human life, that is, death. This is so even when the rest of the body, including the spinal cord, skeletal muscles, and the heart, are still functioning. Indeed, under this condition of brain death, the other organs or tissues may be taken for transplantation to other people.

In earlier times, the heart was often regarded as the seat of consciousness and of emotional feelings (see Aristotle). But replacing one heart with another (even one that is a mechanical device) does not alter an individual's emotional makeup or experience.

So, what sorts of factual answers to the questions about conscious experience could we hope to pursue successfully, and what answers have we now achieved? One important question—how brain activities are related to conscious and unconscious mental function—is, in principle, amenable to descriptive and experimental investigation. But to do that, we need to define conscious subjective experience, and do so in a way that is operational—that is, practical for study.

We start with the stubborn fact that a conscious subjective experience is directly accessible only to the individual who has the experience. Consequently, the only valid evidence for an external observer must come from an introspective report of the experience by the subject.

## Introspective Reports of Subjective Experience

Scientists, like philosophers, have speculated about how the brain and mind are connected. But, until recently, very few, including neuroscientists, have attempted direct experimental studies of how cerebral nerve cell activities are involved in the production or appearance of conscious, subjective experiences. Why? Apart from the technical difficulties for such experiments on human subjects, a philosophical impediment has played a major role.

Studies that require data from introspective reports of subjective experiences have tended to be taboo in the academic community. That negative attitude was influenced in large part by the dominance, during the first seventy-five years of the twentieth century, of behaviorism in psychology and of logical positivism in philosophy. These viewpoints hold that only directly observable events are admissible as scientific data. Introspective reports are only indirectly related to the actual subjective experiences; that is, they are reports of something not directly observable by the investigator and are untrustworthy observations. However, unless scientists can find a way to obtain valid introspective reports, they can never study the profoundly important question of how our conscious mind is related to our brain. The late great physicist Richard Feynman stated, "I'm just looking to find out more about the world . . . Whatever way it comes out, it's nature, and she is going to come out the way she is! Therefore, when we go to investigate it we shouldn't pre-decide what it is we're going to find."

We must, of course, admit that an introspective report does not provide absolute evidence about the experience. (Parenthetically, physicists agree that even hard-nosed physical measurements cannot be made with absolute certainty.) The only subjective experience that one can be absolutely certain about is one's own experience—as noted by René Descartes, Bishop Berkeley, and others. Yet, in our ordinary social interactions we commonly accept introspective reports of experiences by other individuals as meaningful reflections of their experiences, although we may try to evaluate the validity of these reports.

To be sure, the conversion and transmission of an experience into a report may involve some distortion. However, it is possible to limit the kinds of experiences being studied to very simple ones that do not have emotional content. These experiences can even be tested for reliability. In our own investigations we used very simple sensory experiences that had no emotional aspects that might lead to distortion. Furthermore, we could test the reliability of the reports, by changing the sensory inputs in ways under the investigator's control and comparing the different reports elicited in this way. It should have been clear, therefore, that a way to study subjective experiences scientifically can be achieved.

I should add that an introspective report need not be made by a verbal, oral statement. A nonverbal report, like tapping an appropriate key to indicate whether a sensation had been subjectively felt, can be quite acceptable, providing the subject understands that this indicator in fact refers to a subjective, introspective experience.

I may add here that when I was an undergraduate, I realized that verbal expressions are not completely adequate representations of reality. They are only approximations, limited by the meanings attributable to the words. I decided, therefore, to try to think about reality in a nonverbal way—that is, to try to grasp the real situation in a fully integrated and intuitive way. In my subsequent thinking about experimental problems, I did actually tend to view them in nonverbal ways.

The development of cognitive psychology in the 1970s onward became a major factor in shifting scientific opinion on the usefulness of introspective reports. Cognitive scientists wanted to deal with questions about what people knew and felt, and how that was related to reality. To do so, they had to have people tell them about their subjective experiences. I should note that there are still traditional behaviorists among psychologists, and that a large group of philosophers adhere to a movement related to behaviorism called functionalism.

Starting in the late 1950s, I did not wait for cognitive science to support my use of introspective reports in our studies. I approached this issue as a physiologist, with no stake in behaviorism or functionalism. My attitude was, from the start, that conscious experience could be studied and treated like any other observable function of the brain. As an experimental scientist, it was, and is, my firm conviction that a person's report of a conscious experience should be regarded as primary evidence. This evidence should not be altered or distorted so as to be made to conform to a preconceived view or theory about the nature of consciousness. Unless they can be convincingly affected or contradicted by other evidence, properly obtained introspective reports of conscious experience should be looked on like other kinds of objective evidence.

I was, in fact surprised when I found that a controlling body of opinion among behavioral scientists did not agree with my view. Indeed, a visiting group of such individuals, representing a study section of the National Institutes of Health, told me I was not studying a suitable topic. They denied my application for a grant.

Interestingly, I found no such rejection among the world's

leaders in experimental neurophysiology, such as Lord Adrian, Sir John Eccles, Herbert Jasper, Charles Phillips, Wilder Penfield, Roger Sperry, Frederic Bremer, Ragnar Granit, Anders Lundberg, Robert Doty, and Howard Shevrin. These researchers regarded our work as praiseworthy and pioneering—sentiments also expressed during a major symposium entitled "Brain and Conscious Experience" in 1964. Sponsored by the Pontifical Academy of Sciences and chaired by Sir John Eccles, this symposium was held in the fifteenth-century house of Pius IV, inside the Vatican grounds. Pope Paul took us seriously enough to hold a formal audience with us. The twenty-five or so members of the symposium were seated on one side of a great hall, and a roughly equal number of Cardinals faced us on the other side in their red robes. When the Pope came down to greet us, the Catholic scientists knelt and kissed his ring, and the rest of us shook his hand. I still have the thick red leather nameplate with gold lettering from that meeting. Since then, I have been a participant and speaker in a number of additional interesting symposia on consciousness. There was, in fact, another one in the Vatican in 1988, again organized by Sir John Eccles.

Besides neurophysiologists, leading philosophers such as the late Sir Karl Popper, Thomas Nagel, and the late Stephen Pepper also agree with my views concerning how to study conscious subjective experience. Stephen Pepper was Professor of Philosophy at the University of California–Berkeley. Pepper was a strong advocate of so-called identity theory, which holds that the externally observable physical quality of the brain and the inner quality of subjective experience are simply different phenomenological aspects of a single "substrate." Nevertheless, Pepper listened carefully to my discussion of my team's views and findings; he even concluded that our evidence for a retroactive referral of sensory timing might argue against the validity of identity theory.

## *Awareness*

The use of introspective reports in our studies led me to recognize the nature of their significance more clearly. I realized that the essential feature of introspective reports of conscious experiences is awareness, or being aware of something. *What* one is aware of encompasses a great variety of experiential contents, including awareness of the external world and of our internal bodily world (via sensory inputs), of our feelings (anger, joy, depression), of our thoughts and imaginations, and of our self.

Many, if not most, philosophers have spoken of different kinds and levels of conscious experience. Commonly, self-awareness is regarded as a special case and one that may be limited to human beings and possibly chimpanzees. We cannot be sure that the experiential contents even of similar events are identical in other people. For example, what I see as yellow might not be identical to what you see as yellow, even though we have learned to give that kind of experience the same name. We can be much more confident that the feature of awareness itself, in the other person, is fundamentally identical to our own awareness, even if the contents of that yellow experience may not be identical.

I suggest, therefore, that there is no need to invent different kinds or categories of consciousness or of conscious experiences to deal with all the kinds of experiences. The common feature in all cases is awareness. The differences lie in the different *contents* of awareness. As I will argue from the experimental evidence, awareness *per se* is a unique phenomenon, and it is associated with unique neuronal activities that are a necessary condition for all conscious experiences.

Sensory experiences of pain, color, harmonies, and odors have been called *qualia* by philosophers. Such experiences represent phenomena not explainable by the physical nature of the stimuli that produce them or by the corresponding neural activities, and so they pose difficulties for materialist theories about conscious experience. But I see no reason for setting up these qualia as a problem that is fundamentally different from other awarenesses. Awarenesses of all kinds are equally unexplainable by materialist theories.

We should distinguish between "conscious experiences" and the state of simply being awake and responsive—in other words, being in a "conscious" state. To be in a conscious state is, of course, a prerequisite for the appearance of conscious subjective experiences, except in the case of dreams. In dreaming, we have conscious experiences during the sleep state. However, the state of being awake and conscious, and the phase of sleep during which dreams appear, both require a diffuse activation of the cerebral cortex by structures in the brain stem and in the thalamus (the structure at the base of the forebrain, below the cerebral hemisphere). This function in the brain is a necessary background condition for the production of conscious experiences.

### How Can We Study the Relation between the Brain and Conscious Subjective Experience?

My attitude has always been the same: never mind the speculative untested theories. Rather, focus on finding out how the brain *actually* deals with or brings about the appearance of a conscious experience. I suppose this attitude stems from my background in experimental neurophysiology. Our goal is to discover how the nervous system works in producing the behaviors of the individual, based on evidence.

A major difficulty for such investigations is the need for human subjects—with whom direct studies of brain functions are, of course, severely limited. Much can be done with animals at a behavioral level for work on memory and learning, representation of visual processes (spatial, colors), and so on. But all of such functions can be performed *without* conscious awareness, as they can be even in human subjects. As Marion Stamp Dawkins put it, One should take care not to "blur the important distinction between being clever and being conscious." That is, we should be on guard against "the impression that all we need to do to probe animal (or human) minds is to show they are capable of various complex intellectual tasks and we will inevitably have shown that they are conscious" (in other words, subjectively aware).

Only recently has an experimental design been devised (by Stoerig and Cowey, 1995) that can generate some confidence that a monkey is employing conscious awareness in order to perform a subtle task. This design involved monkeys with lesions of the primary visual cortex. The same lesions in humans result in a loss of conscious vision, or blindness. Visual stimuli were presented and the monkeys' ability to detect these stimuli was tested. When a monkey had to give a forced choice response (yes or no), stimuli presented in the defective "blind" visual field were detected 100 percent of the time. Human patients with a similar defect in the visual cortex can point correctly to a target, though they claim they cannot see it (a phenomenon called "blindsight"). But when a monkey was allowed to respond freely, it classified such stimuli in the defective visual field as "blanks," in other words, nothing there. In this condition, the monkey appeared to be communicating, "I don't consciously see anything in that blind visual field." That result supports the view that the monkeys in this experiment could distinguish between conscious vision and unconscious detection.

For our experimental approach to the question of how to study the relationship between the brain and conscious subjective experience, I set out two epistemological principles that I believe must be followed: the introspective report as the operational criterion and no *a priori* rules for mind-brain relationship.

**1. *Introspective report as the operational criterion.*** I have already discussed the case for introspective reports. Here is an important corollary of this principle: Any behavioral evidence that does not require a convincing introspective report cannot be assumed to be an indicator of conscious subjective experience. This is so regardless of the purposeful nature of the action or of the complexity of cognitive and abstract problem-solving processes; both can and often do proceed unconsciously without awareness by the subject. One must even be careful to distinguish between the ability to detect a signal and the awareness of the signal.

Behavioral actions are the observable muscle actions and autonomic changes (in heart rate, blood pressure, sweating, and so on). Purely behavioral actions that are *not* reporting an introspective experience cannot provide valid evidence of a conscious *subjective* experience. In reporting an introspective experience, the subject is responding to a question about her private experience and we are confident that she understands the question. A behavioral act made without this condition may, in fact, be performed unconsciously.

**2. *No a priori rules for mind-brain relationship.*** A corollary question is, Can one describe what a person is feeling or thinking (in other words, his subjective experience) by examining the nerve cell activities in the brain without any introspective report by the person? The answer is no. If you were to look into the active brain and observe the multifarious activities of nerve cells in the various structures, you would see nothing that looks like a mental or conscious phenomenon. This point was already made by the great seventeenth-century philosopher and mathematician Leibniz, among others.

In contrast, another great mathematician, Laplace, became enamored of the new mechanistic models in Newton's physics. Laplace proposed that if he could know all the positions and states of energy or motion of all the molecules in the universe, he could predict all future events. He argued that knowledge of all such molecular features in the brain would enable him to specify and predict what was going on mentally. First, this proposition is not testable in practice. Not only can we not hope to specify the data for the astronomically large number of molecules in the brain, but modern physics tells us that it is impossible, in principle, to measure the position and motion simultaneously for any particle. Second, even if we could satisfy Laplace's condition, we would see only molecular configurations, not any mental phenomena. It is curious that a substantial group of philosophers, the functionalists, still hold a behavioristic, Laplacean-like view.

The general principle to be followed, in contrast to behaviorism, is that externally observable "physical" events and the inner observable "mental" events are phenomenologically independent categories. The two are certainly *interrelated,* but the relationship between them can be discovered only by simultaneous observations of the two separate phenomena. The relationship cannot be predicted *a priori. Neither phenomenon is reducible to or describable by the other.*

Take one simple example: Following the electrical stimulation of the cortical area that receives sensory information from the body, the subject does not feel any sensation located in the brain. Instead, he reports feeling something in a part of his body, like the hand, even though nothing actually occurred in the hand. An external observer would have no way of describing this subjective experience without asking the subject for an introspective report about it.

This principle leads to a flat rejection of the reductionist view popular with many scientists and philosophers (for example, Churchland, 1981; Dennett and Kinsbourne, 1992). According to this view, knowledge of the neuronal structures and functions (or their molecular underpinnings) is sufficient for defining and explaining consciousness and mental activities. But we have just seen how that reductionist view would not work.

### Where in the Brain Are the Processes Related to Conscious Experience?

The eminent neurosurgeon Wilder Penfield, with his colleagues (especially Herbert Jasper), made thousands of observations of patients' introspective reports in response to local electrical stimuli to the cerebral cortex. (The cortex was exposed and tested during therapeutic procedures to identify foci of epileptic seizures. Patients were awake, with local anesthetics applied to the scalp.) Other neurosurgeons also carried out such mapping of responses. Reports of sensations were obtained by stimulating the primary sensory areas of the cerebral cortex, whether somatosensory (bodily sensations), visual, or auditory. Clearly, electrical stimulation of the primary sensory cortex would be a good place to study the requirements for producing a conscious, reportable event.

Much of the cerebral cortex does not give conscious responses of any kind when electrically stimulated. But the nerve cells in these "silent" areas do respond to stimuli: Electrical responses (direct cortical responses, or DCRs) are recordable near all stimulus sites. Presumably, the production of a reportable conscious response in silent areas may require more complex activations than are possible at the primary sensory areas of the cortex. Or, silent areas may not mediate conscious functions.

In any case, it is worth emphasizing, from this and other evidence, that considerable amounts of neuronal activity can occur without eliciting any conscious experience.

Penfield and Jasper were impressed by the observation that large destructive lesions in the cerebral hemispheres did not result in loss of consciousness, while small lesions in the activating systems, located in the brain stem or in the intralaminar nuclei of the thalamus, did produce a loss of consciousness, a coma. Penfield (1958) therefore proposed that the "seat" of consciousness is located in these medially situated subcortical structures, which he called the centrencephalic system. Similarly, another eminent neurosurgeon, Joseph Bogen (1995), recently proposed that the conscious function resides in the intralaminar nucleus of the thalamus, a component of the centrencephalic system.

The logical difficulty with Penfield's and Bogen's view is that it does not distinguish between necessary and sufficient conditions. That is, even if a structure is necessary to the conscious function, that does not, in itself, make that structure a sufficient condition for producing conscious experience. There are indeed many other functions that are necessary for the possible production of conscious experience. For example, if the heart stops beating, a person loses all conscious functions within a few seconds. But the heart is not where conscious functions reside, contrary to the notions of many earlier peoples; one can replace a heart with a transplant from someone else or even with a mechanical device and not alter the subject's conscious processes or personality. Furthermore, there is, indeed, much evidence for the view that specific kinds of neuronal activities in the cerebral hemispheres underlie production of conscious events.

A variety of studies have given us important information about where in the brain there are nerve cell activities associated with conscious or behavioral events. These fall into two groups: neuropsychological studies and techniques for measuring changes in brain nerve cell activities.

1. Neuropsychological studies have examined changes in mental functions produced by destructive lesions in specific brain localities. The "granddaddy" in this field is perhaps the case of Phineas Gage, who sustained accidental damage to a frontal portion of both cerebral hemispheres. As he was laying railroad tracks, a metal rod was accidentally propelled into one side of Gage's head, in front of the temporal lobe; the rod went right through to the other side of his head. Gage survived, but his personality changed dramatically. Previously a stable, reliable, and sociable person, he became uninhibited (swearing freely and easily aroused emotionally), unreliable in his work, and deficient in foresight and planning. His case highlights the importance of the frontal lobes of the brain in functions of self-control, planning, and so on. Much more has since been discovered about functions of the frontal lobes.

More recently, neuropsychologists have been developing representations of subtle differences in mental functions about which we had no previous inklings. For example, certain specific lesions produced by local damage from blood clots or bleeding (in other words, small strokes) can produce the inability to detect consonants in spoken words although the vowels remain understandable. As a result, patients are almost completely unable to grasp spoken words.

2. A variety of techniques can measure local changes in the intensity of nerve cell activities in the brain. These techniques are based on the premise that an increase in local neural activity is accompanied by an increase in the energy metabolism of the nerve cells. That increase in metabolism could result in a higher local consumption of oxygen and the release of certain end-products of metabolism into the local spaces around those nerve cells. Most notably, oxidation of glucose produces carbon dioxide ($CO_2$). $CO_2$ is known to produce a dilation of the small arterioles, thereby increasing the circulating blood in that area.

The first successful technique for measuring changes in local or regional cerebral blood flow (rCBF) was devised by the Swedish clinical neurophysiologist David Ingvar and his colleagues (see Lassen and Ingvar, 1961; Ingvar, 1979, 1999). In principle, the technique involves measuring and mapping local changes in radioactivity, after an injection of a relatively safe dose of a radioactive compound into the cerebral blood supply. A large number of scintillation counters are arranged on the subject's scalp; each of these counts the radioactive emissions at its site and thus records the degree of radioactivity of the injected compound in its locality. An increase in the radioactivity at certain calibrated times after the injection indicates an increase in the circulating blood carrying it into that region.

Ingvar and his colleagues studied changes in rCBFs not only with sensory inputs and motor activities but also with thought processes. They found, for example, that if a subject simply imagined moving her fingers, without actually moving them, increases in rCBF could be detected in some of the same areas that "lit up" when subjects moved their fingers voluntarily. Further studies (Roland and Friberg, 1985) showed activation of cortical fields (especially in frontal lobe) with thinking involving silent subtraction of numbers; this activation occurred with no activations of sensory or motor areas.

One could argue that such results are evidence of the ability of a conscious mental process to influence neuronal activity in the brain. One could also study pathological conditions to look for local or general abnormalities in cerebral circulation, whether in the resting state or in response to relevant stimuli or tasks. For example, certain deficiencies in blood circulating in the brain have been observed in people with early Alzheimer's disease, schizophrenia, and other health issues.

Louis Sokoloff and his team (1977) pioneered improved measurement of local metabolic changes in the intact brain. That work led directly to the invention of more powerful methods to detect changes in metabolism. As with the Ingvar technique, no surgical penetrations into the brain were required so these methods could be used in human subjects. The two methods widely in use at present improved both the spatial refinement and the speed of measurement.

The first of these methods is positron-emission-tomography (PET scans). This method involves injecting weakly radioactive substances that emit positrons, instead of electromagnetic radiations. The positrons are detected by a large number of small devices arranged on the scalp.

The second method uses magnetic resonance imaging (MRI) to show quantitative changes in a variety of atoms (such as oxygen and carbon) associated with the neural functions, in a highly localized fashion.

All of these investigations—studies in neuropsychology, rCBFs, PET scans, functional MRIs—give us information only about *where* in the brain the nerve cell activities may be related to various mental operations. They do not tell us what kinds of nerve cell activities (changes in local patterns, frequencies of firing, and so on), are involved. Nor do they sufficiently indicate the timing in the relation between changes in nerve cell activities and a mental function (such as the relation between the timing of a change in brain activity relative to conscious awareness of a given event). Indeed, it is even possible that the areas showing increased activity are not the sites of primary importance in the initiation or organization of the functions being tested. The primary sites could be smaller and show much weaker changes in the measured images.

Even when one of these methods becomes capable of very fast resolution of changes in time, as the functional MRIs have become, estimation of the timing of the neural changes is limited by the physiological process being measured. The MRI method (like the PET scan) measures a change in local circulation of blood or in chemical constituents produced by a metabolic change in the nerve cells. Such metabolic changes mostly *follow* the functionally relevant changes in the nerve cells (whether these are synaptic responses or alterations in firing of nerve impulses). The important relevant changes in activity of the nerve cells can occur in milliseconds; but the metabolic energy changes, initiated by these neural activities, may take seconds to produce the changes that are measurable by these techniques. Thus, it is not possible to answer questions such as, Does conscious intention precede or follow the cerebral initiation of a voluntary act?

### Electrophysiology

The recording of electrical events that are an intrinsic component of the relevant neuronal activities does allow us to achieve virtually instantaneous indicators of changes in nerve cell activities. These recordings result from fields of electric current (and voltage) that are set up both by the actual firing of conducting nerve impulses (by their *action potentials*), and by the more local, nonconducting *synaptic potentials*. Synaptic potentials are produced when fibers coming from other nerve cells deliver an incoming message to their terminals, where they make contact with specialized areas of the surface membrane of the next nerve cell. The specialized junction between the incoming fiber and the site where it terminates on another cell is called a *synapse*(from the Greek for clasping of two elements). In most synapses the incoming terminal can release a special chemical, a neurotransmitter. The area of cell membrane on the receiving side of the synapse contains receptors specialized to respond to the neurotransmitter.

The postsynaptic response usually results in a local electrical change, making the external side of the receiving membrane either more negative (with excitatory effects), or more positive (with inhibitory effects). In either case, a difference in electrical potential (voltage) is thus created between the local postsynaptic portion of cell membrane and the adjacent membrane (not similarly affected) of that same cell. That produces a field of electric current around the cell. The voltage changes in that electric field can best be detected by an electrode placed in the external medium close to the cell. However, smaller voltages of that field can be recorded at greater distances, using suitable amplifiers.

Thus, very small voltages, in the microvolt range, can be detected even on the scalp. These are the basis of the electroencephalogram (EEG; also called the "brain waves"). These EEG electrical rhythms were first reported in humans by Hans Berger in 1929. The EEG is now widely used in studies of brain functions in both normal and clinical conditions. For example, typical changes in brain waves accompany the transitions from the waking state to various states of sleep. And typical changes that accompany epileptic activity are used to diagnose and locate the site of epileptic foci.

Magnetoencephalograms (MEGs) have also come into use recently. These are recordings of the small magnetic fields generated by electrical currents. MEGs, recorded with detectors at the scalp, are claimed to give better indicators of the originating neural fields than do EEGs. However, small electrodes introduced intracranially to make direct contact with the cortical surface or inserted into deeper subcortical structures can detect electrical changes that are more localized and more meaningful than any scalp recording, whether EEG or MEG.

It is possible, and often desirable, to perform some neurosurgical procedures without general anesthesia in an awake patient. To accomplish this, a local anesthetic is injected into the scalp and tissues covering the cranial bone. That procedure is sufficient to block any pain, as no pain is generated by drilling a hole in the cranial bone or by making contacts with brain tissues. There are no special nerve endings that respond to injury in the brain, such as those that respond to injury elsewhere and that lead to feeling pain when these messages reach certain places in the brain. Pain is very important for informing us of tissue injury, so that we can try to get away from the source of injury. Presumably, there is no adaptive value for such a warning system in the brain itself. The brain is encased in a protective bony cranium. Any object that could produce injury to the brain would first produce pain when it penetrates the scalp and linings of the bone, as well as the membranes (meninges) that cover the brain. However, an injurious tumor growing within the brain

does not produce pain and is therefore an insidious and dangerous agent of injury.

The American neurosurgeon Harvey Cushing (1909) was one
of the first to show that electrical stimulation of the appropriate
sensory cortex could evoke reports of tingling sensations by the
subject. (This was before the days of electrical recordings here.)
When the stimulating electrode was placed on the postcentral
gyrus (the rounded surface lying behind the central "Rolandic"
fissure of the cerebral cortex), a tingling sensation was felt in
some part of the body. It was not felt at the stimulated area of
the brain. Stimulation of the precentral gyrus, just in front of
the fissure, produced local movements of various parts of the
body. These areas then comprised the primary somatosensory
area and primary motor area of the cerebral cortex.

Somewhat later, the German neurosurgeon Otfrid Foerster
(referenced in Penfield, 1958) and the American-Canadian neurosurgeon Wilder Penfield greatly expanded the knowledge ob-
tainable this way (see Penfield and Boldrey, 1937). They can-
vassed virtually the whole cortical surface, in various patients.
They, and others since, found that stimulation of most areas of
the cortex produced no reportable sensations, movements, or
feelings; these areas were called "silent." The "excitable" areas
that did produce responses were limited to the so-called primary
sensory areas for bodily and somatic sensations, the visual one
(in a defined area at the occipital, rear pole of the cortex) and
the auditory cortex (on the upper forward area of the temporal
lobe). Penfield also observed psychic reports of hallucinations,
memories, and so on when he stimulated some areas of the
temporal lobe. (Indeed the temporal lobe with its subcortical
structures—hippocampus and amygdala—is now regarded as an
important mediator of memory formation and certain emotional feelings, particularly of fear and aggression.)

Stimulation of the silent areas was shown, by us and others, to produce electrical evidence of considerable responsiveness by nerve cells locally. Why then is there no subjective report from the subject? I proposed that the crude excitation of local bundles of nerve fibers would be unlikely to lead to the kind of organized activities that may be necessary to activate a subjective experience. Indeed we are lucky that stimulation of the "primary" sensory and motor areas can elicit subjective responses. We can only guess that happens because the nerve fibers excited in those localities have sufficient access to nerve cells directly mediating these subjective responses.

On the other hand, electrical stimulation of the silent areas in animals (cats, monkeys) has been shown (by Robert Doty and others; see Doty, 1969), to participate as part of a conditioned reflex (CR). In an ordinary CR, an effective unconditioned stimulus (US) produces a natural response that requires no learning. For example, a mild shock to a paw (the US) causes the animal to withdraw its paw. If an unrelated conditional stimulus (CS) is applied in less than 1 sec before the US, the animal learns to withdraw the paw when that CS (say an auditory tone) is applied alone. An electrical stimulus to silent cortex can act like a more conventional CS, equivalent to sounding a tone. That is, the animal can learn to withdraw its paw when that cortical stimulus was given alone. This and other evidence indicates that a specific activation of neurons in almost any part of the cerebral cortex can be detected by a subject in a functionally effective manner. Such detection of electrically activated neural responses in the silent cerebral cortex is presumably made *unconsciously,* if one extrapolates from the absence of any conscious experiences with similar stimulations in human subjects.

Whether a stimulus to silent cortex in a human subject can also be detected unconsciously is an interesting point that should be experimentally tested. (That is something I wanted to do but was unable to undertake before my retirement.) Our other experimental evidence does show that certain stimuli in the sensory pathway, even when inadequate to produce any conscious experience, can nevertheless be usefully detected by the human subject (Libet et al., 1991; see Chap. 4). The important inference is, then, that neural activities inadequate to produce any subjective experience or awareness can nevertheless help to mediate functions without awareness. Indeed, much of our brain activities are of that nature.

### Our Experimental Entry

My opportunity to get into such studies came from my colleague and friend Dr. Bertram Feinstein. Bert was an experimental neurologist with the Biomechanics Lab at UCSF. I was associated with him there in work on muscle functions related to locomotion. Bert converted to neurosurgery by spending three years of study in the early 1950s, with the great neurosurgeon in Sweden, Lars Leksell.

He then introduced stereotaxic neurosurgery to San Francisco, actually to the western United States (see Feinstein et al., 1960). In stereotaxic neurosurgery, a therapeutic electrode or probe is introduced into the brain, so as to reach a designated deeper structure without cutting the brain open to get there. A frame with coordinates in three dimensions is fixed to the patient's skull. The coordinates for reading the target in the brain are mapped in advance. At that time, the method was mainly used to inactivate certain deep structures, by a heating probe, to relieve tremor in Parkinsonian patients.

The Leksell-type frame permitted Feinstein to reach a targeted structure in the brain by one of a large variety of possible paths. The carrier of the shaft to be inserted into the brain was a hemispheric device that could move to any position from front to back. As a result, he could adopt any angle of entry to reach a given target. He could thus choose a track in which the inserted shaft might go through other structures of research interest on the way to the therapeutic target.

Bert Feinstein was unusual among neurosurgeons in his desire to use such opportunities to study questions of fundamental interest, providing such studies could be done with essentially no added risks to the patient (and, of course, with informed consent of the patient and the approval of the hospital committee overseeing human experiments.)

When Feinstein offered me the opportunity to devise worthwhile basic studies for which intracranial access to the brain of awake subjects was required, I immediately decided we should try to find out how activities in the brain are related to or produce a conscious experience. This question was one that could not be pursued in nonhuman animals, because animals cannot give introspective reports of subjective experience.

The pursuit of how brain activities relate to or produce conscious experience had been a long-range goal of mine. I was fascinated by the question of how our conscious subjective experience could arise in the brain. I did my graduate school research on the electrophysiological activities of the isolated frog brain with the eminent neuroscientist Ralph Gerard, my professor at the University of Chicago. Gerard asked me, at one point during my first year with him, to make a list of my views of what the spontaneous electrical brain waves were doing for the frog. One item I put down was that these waves might be a neural expression for consciousness of the frog! Gerard had a broad integrated view of brain functions, and he was open to any views and comments that I made. I was lucky to have been associated with him in that research.

To facilitate the studies, for both clinical and basic experimental purposes, Feinstein had a new operating room constructed at the Mt. Zion Hospital in San Francisco. This room was electrically shielded and contained conduits for electrical recording of nerve cell activities in the brain and for delivering electrical stimuli. The conduits went to an adjacent control room for the electrical equipment and operators of that equipment.

Our studies during the initial several years, beginning in 1958, were made during neurosurgical procedures in the operating room (see Libet et al., 1964). The patients were awake, with only a local anesthetic applied to the scalp and to the periosteal tissue covering the bone of the skull. Each patient had, of course, previously given an informed consent for the essentially risk-free experimental procedure, which included a provision for the patient to terminate the study at any time. Patients were generally remarkably cooperative and consistent in their responses. However, we were limited to about thirty minutes of study in the operating room. It was, therefore, essential to have the study thoroughly organized and planned for an efficient and productive session. We needed a period of relaxed rest afterward, to cool off from the concentrated discipline of the procedure.

The study sessions became more relaxed and fruitful when Feinstein altered the therapeutic procedure in the 1960s. He preferred leaving the inserts in the brain for some days or a week, to allow the therapeutic lesions to be made in stages with the patient in a more normal, ambulatory state. That procedural change permitted us to study the patients more fully and at a more leisurely pace outside the operating room. Later, Feinstein treated patients who suffered from intractable pain by placing stimulating electrodes permanently in the sensory pathway below the cerebral cortex. We were then able to study these patients at length, even during return visits to Dr. Feinstein.

Feinstein died prematurely in 1978. I lost a dear friend and the world lost a pioneer in experimental neurosurgery. His death also changed the direction of my research. I turned to a study of how conscious will is related to brain functions. That study could be carried out with normal subjects. Recording electrodes on the scalp were sufficient for detecting the electrical changes accompanying a voluntary act, and that was what I needed for the experiment I had designed. (See Chap. 4 for a full description.)

Of course, even with the cooperation of a neurosurgeon like Feinstein and of suitable subjects, the number of available subjects for complete studies was severely limited. But the logic of even single-case studies can be argued, as discussed by John C. Marshall (1989) in his review of the book by Tim Shallice (*From Neuropsychology to Mental Structure,* 1989). Claude Bernard (the great physiologist of the late 1800s) argued that the use of group averages in medicine and physiology "leads necessarily to error." And Bernard was quoted, in support, on a study in which a physiologist "took urine from a railroad station where people of all nations passed, and who believed he could thus present an analysis of average European urine. . . . If we have learned anything it is that only the fine detail of a patient's performance that suffices for model building, and that, at this level, theoretically important individual variation is paramount."

The rest of this book is oriented around the unique experimental developments and discoveries we were fortunately able to make on the great fundamental issue: How are nerve cell activities in the brain related to conscious subjective experience and to unconscious mental functions? I also allude to other studies as they impinge directly on the implications of our discoveries.

I hope that you, the reader, will see how we designed and experimentally tested hypotheses that were generated to explain new findings, and that you will be able to share in this story of scientific inquiry and in the excitements and thrills of these discoveries. In contrast to most other books about consciousness, you are about to be exposed to *direct experimental evidence* and to *testable theories on this issue,* rather than to speculative and mostly nontested constructions.

# 2

## THE DELAY IN OUR CONSCIOUS SENSORY AWARENESS

If you tap your finger on a table, you experience the event as occurring in "real time." That is, you subjectively feel the touch occurring at the same time that your finger makes contact with the table. But our experimental evidence strongly supports a surprising finding that is directly counter to our own intuition and feelings: The brain needs a relatively long period of appropriate activations, up to about half a second, to elicit awareness of the event! Your conscious experience or awareness of your finger touching the table thus appears only after the brain activities have become adequate to produce the awareness.

We are talking here about *actual awareness* of a signal, which must be clearly distinguished from the *detection* of a signal. For example, human and nonhuman beings can discriminate between two different frequencies of tactile vibration, even though the intervals between two pulses in each vibration frequency are only a few milliseconds (msec) in length. A leading neuroscientist criticized our discovery of an interval of up to 500 msec before a conscious experience appeared, on just these grounds. If we can differentiate between vibrating frequencies in which successive pulses are separated by a few milliseconds, how could we propose an interval of up to 500 msec before awareness of such short intervals between pulses? My reply was that the ability to detect differences in millisecond intervals is undeniable, but when is one *aware* of that detection? Becoming consciously aware of the difference is what requires the relatively long time. In other words, detection leading to some response can occur *unconsciously,* without any awareness of the signal.

If such physiological delays are built into the brain's production of sensory awareness, a number of profound questions and implications arise: Why do we feel as though we are immediately aware of an event, as if there were no delay in our actual awareness? What about our abilities to react to a sensory stimulus within 100 msec or so, a delay much shorter than needed for awareness? For example, is a competitive runner aware of the sound of the starting gun when she takes off in a race within much less than 0.5 sec? Do unconscious mental functions have a different time requirement than conscious mental functions?

To be convinced of this unexpected and counterintuitive delay in awareness, you need to see the evidence. The following sections outline the kinds of observations we made and how these led to the surprising discovery of a delay in awareness.

### Initial Evidence from Cerebral Stimulation

In 1957 or so, my collaborator and friend, neurosurgeon Dr. Bertram Feinstein, invited me to design and carry out experiments that could be done while he performed surgical treatments on the brain, and to do so in a way that introduced no new risks and was acceptable to the patient. I jumped at this wonderful opportunity to investigate what the brain must do in order to produce a conscious experience.

Perhaps the most difficult part of the research enterprise reared its head at its beginning, in 1957–1958. How could we begin the experimental approach to the issue of brain processes for conscious experience? What significant question could we ask that was also amenable to experimental study, especially within the limitations of access time to the subject and to the brain structures available for study?

At the start, we had available electrode contacts sitting on the surface of the primary somatosensory cortex (Fig. 2.1). This is the area of cerebral cortex that receives the direct sensory input from all areas of the body and skin. It was also known that electrical stimulation applied to the surface of this area could, in a subject who was awake, elicit a conscious sensation of localized tingling or other responses. These sensations were reported by the subjects as coming from some specific skin or body structure, not from the brain. That is, the sensation is "referred" subjectively to some bodily structure that normally sends its sensory input to the spot of the cortex being stimulated.

Fortunately, we began with a relatively simple question, which led to some significant answers. The initial experimental question became: What kinds of activations of neurons in this sensory area are critical to production of just threshold conscious sensation, that is, the weakest reportable conscious sensation? The relevant neuronal activations could be evaluated from the effective electrical stimulations, and from the recordable electrical changes produced by the nerve cells.

The big advantage in studying this question by stimulating the brain itself was that we might find requirements at the cerebral level that are obscured by stimulation of the skin. It was already known that a sensory input from the skin can result in messages that ascend to the brain in several different spinal cord pathways.

A

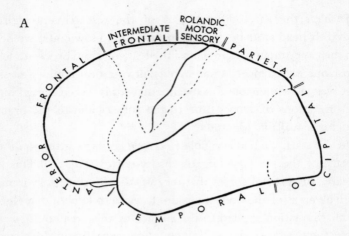

B

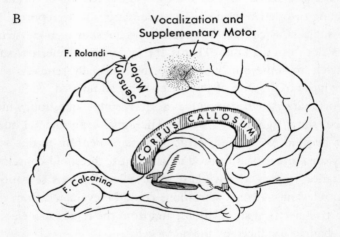

**Fig. 2.1.** Maps of human cerebral cortex.

A. Lateral view of left hemisphere. Rolandic fissure separates the frontal
and parietal lobes. The anterior, frontal side of Rolandic fissure contains
the primary motor area (MI); nerve cells in this area send motor nerve
fibers directly to the final motor-neurones that directly activate skeletal
muscles. The posterior area behind the Rolandic fissure contains the primary somatosensory area (SI). Nerve cells in this area receive the fastest
sensory nerve fibers that originate in the skin, tendons, and muscles.

Primary receiving area for auditory input is at the upper margin of the
temporal lobe. Primary visual area is at the rear (posterior) tip of the occipital lobe.

B. Medial side of the left hemisphere. This side is at midline, facing the

C

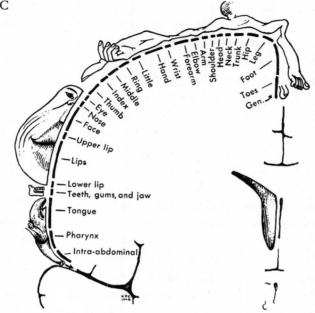

medial side of the right hemisphere. The frontal region is to the right here, turned 180° from that in Fig. 2.1A.

The top end of the Rolandic fissure is visible, as it continues a bit over into the medial side.

Frontal or anterior to the end of MI is the supplementary motor area (SMA). Electrical stimulation of the SMA can produce general bodily movements or vocalizations. The SMA appears to be involved in the preparation and initiation of a voluntary act (see Chapter 4).

The corpus callosum is the massive bridge of nerve fibers that carry messages between the two hemispheres. It has been cut through here in order to separate the two hemispheres for this medial view.

The calcarine fissure, at the occipital pole (on the left here), marks the location of most of the primary visual receiving area.

C. The sensory "homunculus." Representation of the right side of body in the primary somatosensory area of the left cerebral cortex. The figurine is laid upon a cross-section of the hemisphere at the level of SI sensory cortex. From Penfield and Rasmussen, 1950.

For both MI and SI, the opposite side of the body is represented (the right side for this left hemisphere). Also, the body is represented upside down. That is, the head and face are at the bottom, and the legs and feet at the top of each area. From Penfield and Rasmussen, 1950. Reprinted with permission from The Gale Group.

That can result in a variety of modified messages that arrive at higher brain levels, producing an unknown variety of activations there. In fact, we would not have been able to discover the cerebral delay for awareness if we had been limited to peripheral sensory input, from the skin in this case.

Another important experimental strategy was to focus on studying changes at the level for producing a just threshold sensory experience. That is, we looked for the differences in the brain activities between two conditions: 1) when the stimulus input was still too low to produce any sensory awareness, and 2) when the input was raised to a level that just begins to elicit the weakest reportable subjective sensation. This strategy had two important benefits. First, it was clear that a normally functioning brain is necessary before any special neuronal activities will lead to a subjective sensation. With our approach, we avoided having to deal with the enormously complex necessary background of brain activity. Instead, we focused on the cerebral events critical to the appearance of awareness, starting from that general necessary background. Second, study of the changeover from no-awareness to the awareness of a sensory stimulus could give potential insights into what cerebral activities may mediate *unconscious* or nonconscious mental functions. (This later developed into an experimental study of the different requirements for unconscious versus conscious mental functions.)

So, what did we find, from applying all kinds of variations of the stimulus to the sensory cortex? (See Libet et al., 1964; Libet, 1973.) The stimulus consisted of brief pulses of current (each about 0.1 to 0.5 msec in duration, in different experiments), repeated at 20 or 60 pulses per second. A time factor turned out to be the most interesting requirement for eliciting a conscious sensation. To elicit a report of a weak, threshold-level sensation, the repetitive stimulus pulses had to continue for about 0.5 sec. That requirement was surprisingly long for a neural function.

How was this measured? With a long 5-sec *train* of those pulses, the intensity (strength of current in each pulse) had to be raised to some minimum *(liminal)* level in order to produce the weakest conscious sensation (see Fig. 2.2A). When this liminal intensity train of pulses was shortened below 5 sec, the duration of the conscious sensation, as reported by the subject, was also shortened. But the perceived strength of the sensation was not changed. Finally, when the liminal stimulus train was shortened to below 0.5 sec, the sensation vanished. Short trains (less than 0.5 sec) could, however elicit a conscious sensation if the intensity (peak current) of the pulses was raised sufficiently (see Fig. 2.2B). But the higher intensities got into a range that is probably not often encountered in a person's normal everyday level of peripheral sensory input.

How does raising the stimulus intensity make it possible for trains of pulses shorter than 0.5 sec to become effective? A higher intensity would undoubtedly excite a greater number of nerve fibers and affect a larger number of nerve cells that receive input from these fibers. Alternatively, that raising of intensity could result in an increase in the frequency of firing by many of the same neurons that responded to the lower, liminal intensity of stimulus. In this connection, a higher frequency of *stimulus* pulses—for example, changing from 30 pulses per second (pps) to 60 pps—resulted in a lowering of the liminal intensity. But there was *no change* in the *minimum train duration* of 0.5 sec required by the 60 pps to elicit a conscious sensation (see Fig. 2.2B). That indicates that the minimum requirement of a 0.5-sec train duration is independent of the frequency or the number of

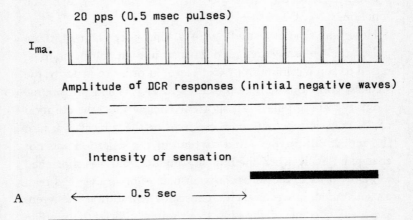

THRESHOLD STIMULUS TRAIN FOR CONSCIOUS SENSATION

20 pps (0.5 msec pulses)

$I_{ma.}$

Amplitude of DCR responses (initial negative waves)

Intensity of sensation

A

← 0.5 sec →

**Fig. 2.2.** Duration of stimulus train of pulses, relative to production of conscious somatic sensation.

A. Diagram of a train of 0.5-msec electrical pulses, at the liminal intensity for eliciting any sensation, applied to cortical area SI, postcentral gyrus. From Libet, 1966.

Second line plots the amplitudes of the direct cortical responses (DCRs) recordable with each pulse.

Third line indicates that no reportable conscious sensation is elicited until the initial 0.5 sec of pulses has been delivered. The weak sensation begun after the 0.5-sec time continues at the same subjective intensity while the stimulus train continues. (This is in contrast to stimulation of the motor cortex, MI; a motor response starts well before a 0.5-sec duration of stimulus, and it builds up in strength as the stimulus continues.)

B. Stimulus train durations at intensities required for a threshold sensation to appear. (Diagram projected from data for many subjects.) Note there is a minimum train duration of around 0.5 sec (the utilization TD) required for the minimally effective intensity to elicit a sensation. The single pulse usually elicited a motor twitch in the related body part (like the hand or forearm). From Libet, 1973.

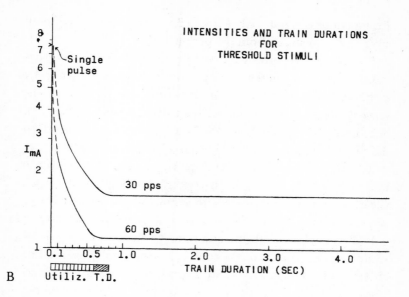

INTENSITIES AND TRAIN DURATIONS
FOR
THRESHOLD STIMULI

Single
pulse

$I_{mA}$

30 pps

60 pps

0.1    0.5    1.0         2.0         3.0         4.0

Utiliz. T.D.

TRAIN DURATION (SEC)

B

stimulus pulses, if the liminal intensity for a given frequency is used.

Raising the stimulus intensity could introduce a complicating factor, in that different nerve fibers of smaller diameters could be fired. How that might affect the responses of the receiving neurons is not clear and is difficult to deal with.

A further complication appeared with stimuli to the somatosensory cortex of sufficient intensity to produce a response with only a few or even a single pulse. However, these responses included a slight twitch in a muscle of the hand or arm. So, at these high intensities there was an observable motor response. What the patients reported was then clearly related to this muscular twitch, which generated an actual peripheral sensory message from receptors in or around the muscle. These motor responses made it impossible to tell whether a single or a few strong pulses could directly elicit a conscious sensation (without any sensory feedback from the periphery).

The motor response to a strong stimulus to the somatosensory cortex is different from the one we obtained by directly stimulating the primary motor cortex (located in front of the sensory area). A few strong pulses to the sensory cortex produced repetitive slight twitches. The same stimuli delivered to the primary motor cortex produced a smooth contraction (not twitches), and this contraction could rapidly rise in strength and eventually into a seizure with continued repetition of pulses. Clearly, the motor responses with stimulation of sensory cortex were not due to electrical spread to the adjacent motor cortex.

We were able to settle the question of whether a strong single stimulus pulse could elicit a conscious sensation when we had an electrode contact located in the ascending sensory pathway below the cerebral cortex. A strong localized pulse here did not elicit any motor response, and a 0.5-sec train of much weaker pulses did elicit a sensation. In other words, some substantial duration of repetitive pulses is necessary to produce a conscious sensation; a single pulse is completely ineffective for that, no matter how strong (when no muscle twitch is produced).

The requirement of some repetition of stimulus pulses to the somatosensory cortex for production of a conscious sensation has been confirmed by several other groups (Grossman, 1980; Tasker, personal communication; Amassian et al., 1991). But our quantitative study established the minimum duration of repetitive liminal intensity pulses at the surprisingly large value of about 0.5 sec. A recent quantitative study of this requirement by Meador and his associates (Ray et al., 1998, 1999) confirmed this value in principle. However, in their case, the minimum duration required at the lowest effective intensity was shorter (almost 0.25 sec) than in our study. One factor in the difference could be Meador's inclusion of epileptic patients in the study. The cortex of such patients can be more excitable than in normal subjects and in the patients we studied.

Is this 0.5-sec requirement unique to the abnormal route of activation, following stimulation at the surface of sensory cortex? The answer was no. The nerve fibers that carry messages for sensations from the skin, joints, and muscles (with the exception of pain and temperature) proceed up to the brain in a large bundle on the back side of the spinal cord (see Fig. 2.3). They terminate on groups (nuclei) of nerve cells in the lowermost portion of the brain, the medulla oblongata. These nerve cells in the medulla produce nerve fibers that cross over to the other side of the brain and proceed to the forebrain in a bundle called the medial lemniscus (so termed for its location and shape). The crossover is what accounts for the representation of sensations in the side of the cerebral hemisphere opposite to the peripheral origin of the sensory stimulus. (Thus, a stroke that damages the pathway in the left side of the brain results in loss of sensations on the right side of the body. The evolutionary value of this crossover is not clear).

The medial lemniscus fibers terminate on specific groups of nerve cells in a lower part of the base of the forebrain, the *thalamus*. These "ventrobasal" cells in the thalamus send nerve fibers directly to the primary somatosensory cerebral cortex. This somatosensory area is located in a fold, or *gyrus*, just in back of, or posterior to, the main vertical cerebral groove called the *central fissure of Rolando*. The spatial origins of the bodily sensations are maintained in this whole pathway, and they terminate differentially on cells in a specific array for the different body parts (see Fig. 2.1C). The whole sensory pathway is there-

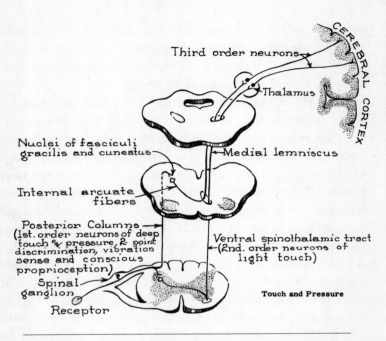

Third order neurons

CEREBRAL CORTEX

Thalamus

Nuclei of fasciculi gracilis and cuneatus

Medial lemniscus

Internal arcuate fibers

Posterior Columns (1st. order neurons of deep touch & pressure, 2 point discrimination, vibration sense and conscious proprioception)

Ventral spinothalamic tract (2nd. order neurons of light touch)

Spinal ganglion

Receptor

**Touch and Pressure**

**Fig. 2.3.** Pathways for the touch, pressure, position-sense sensory nerve fibers from the skin, tendons, and muscles. The fastest of these nerve fibers enter the spinal cord and send a branch directly up in the posterior or dorsal columns of nerve fibers. They end on cells in the medulla, the lowest part of the brain. The nerve fibers from these cells cross over and proceed up in a bundle called the medial lemniscus. These lemniscal fibers end on cells in the ventral-basal thalamus, which then send fibers to end on cells in the somatosensory cortex (SI, in the postcentral gyrus, the cortical fold behind the central Rolandic fissure). The thalamus forms the base of the cerebral hemispheres and has other crucial functions. From Chusid and McDonald, 1958. With permission from the McGraw-Hill Companies.

fore called the *specific projection pathway*, because it retains a specific arrangement of the bodily parts right up to the top. (A similar specificity is seen in the control of muscles by the primary motor area, lying in front of the same central fissure.) The body is represented in an upside-down way, with the legs and feet in the part of the gyrus near the top of the head, and the face and head at its lowest end. So the representation is both crossed over and upside down!

We had some cases in which electrode contacts were located in the thalamic parts of this system and in the medial lemniscus leading into the thalamus. These occurred when the electrodes were placed in these structures for therapeutic purposes. To produce a conscious sensation with electrical stimulations in either of these locations, we found time requirements were the same as they were for the sensory cortex. That is, the train of pulses at the minimally effective intensity had to persist for about 0.5 sec. So, activations in this normal pathway to the cerebral cortex also exhibited the same requirement of a surprisingly long duration of repetitive inputs to elicit a sensory awareness.

This new discovery of the temporal requirement for direct activations at cerebral levels of the sensory pathway, however, seemed not to fit with that for stimuli at the skin, or at nerve fibers from skin into the spinal cord. It has long been known that a conscious sensation can be produced even by a single, weak electrical pulse to the skin (or to the nerve fibers from the skin). So, what goes on here? Is our proposal for a substantial delay in awareness not relevant for normal inputs from the skin?

To look at this question, we had to distinguish between the requirement for a peripheral (skin) input and that for the cerebral processes to which this skin input gives rise. That is, a single effective stimulus pulse to the skin may have to produce a lengthy (0.5-sec) period of cerebral activations before the conscious skin sensation can appear. We therefore looked for ways to test whether this statement is true: Is there a 0.5-sec delay for a conscious sensory awareness even when it is generated by a single pulse input to the skin?

### Actual Delay in Awareness with Normal Sensory Input

Even a single weak pulse to the skin or its sensory nerve is sufficient to elicit a conscious sensation. This statement seems to be counter to the evidence cited in the previous section. In that study we found that up to about 0.5 sec of activations are required to give rise to a conscious sensation. If that applies to the skin stimulus, a single effective stimulus pulse may have to produce a lengthy (0.5-sec) period of cerebral activations before the conscious skin sensation can appear.

So, the next question was: Does the single skin pulse lead to cerebral activations that must persist for about 0.5 sec when that pulse elicits that conscious sensation? That is, is there also an actual delay for sensory awareness when the message is initiated as a single weak pulse applied to normal sources at the skin? This question could only be answered by our distinguishing between the input that is effective at the periphery (skin) and the activations set up by this input at the cerebral level, where the lengthy requirement for awareness is in force. Indeed, we could not have discovered the time factor for awareness if we had been restricted to studying peripheral skin input, rather than direct intracranial input. We were, in fact, able to answer the question we raised in the affirmative, based on three different lines of evidence.

### Electrical Responses of the Cerebral Cortex

The first line of evidence deals with the electrical responses of the cerebral cortex to the single *effective* stimulus pulse to the skin. It had already been demonstrated that each such single pulse gives rise to a sequence of cortical electrical changes, called the evoked potentials (EPs) or the event-related-potentials (ERPs). These ERPs have been shown to represent nerve cell responses in the cortex. They contain a number of differently significant components (see Fig. 2.4). They begin with a primary EP locally produced in the sensory cortex in the specific small area to which the stimulated skin area "projects." The input for the primary EP arrives via the fast specific projection pathway discussed earlier. The primary EP begins after a delay of only some tens of milliseconds after the skin pulse. With a shorter path, say from the hand, it starts after 14–20 msec, while a longer path from the foot may take about 40–50 msec. The size or amplitude of the primary EP is related to the strength of the input from the skin.

A striking feature of the primary EP is that it is neither necessary nor sufficient for eliciting a conscious sensation. We found that it was not necessary because we could elicit a conscious sensation with a weak stimulus applied to the surface of the sensory cortex. This cortical stimulus does not produce any evoked electrical response equivalent to the primary EP; the latter is produced only by input arriving at the cortex from below, via the sensory pathway.

On the other hand, a *single* stimulus pulse in any part of the specific sensory pathway *that is located in the brain* does elicit a primary EP response of the sensory cortex. But this single pulse

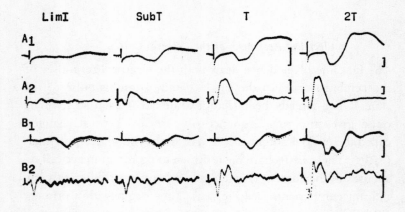

**Fig. 2.4.** Electrical responses (event-related-potentials, ERP) of the cerebral cortex to single stimulus pulses at the skin, averaged from 500 stimulus presentations at 1 per sec.

With just threshold strength stimuli (T) to the hand, virtually all the components of the ERP are already visible. (At T strength not all of the stimuli were felt by the subject.) The initial uptick records the time of the stimulus pulse. About 30 msec later the first response at the SI cortex is a downward, surface-positive deflection, the primary EP. That is followed by later slower components, more pronounced with stimuli at twice threshold strength (2T).

But note that stimulus with subthreshold strength (subT), at 75 percent of T elicits only the primary EP but no later components. (Each whole tracing is 125 msec long in $A_1$ and $B_1$, and 500 msec long in $A_2$ and $B_2$.) From Libet et al., 1967. Reprinted with permission from the American Association for the Advancement of Science.

does not elicit any subjective sensation at all. This is true even when the pulse is relatively strong and the primary EP response it evokes is large (Libet et al., 1967; see Fig. 2.5). An inability of (single) responses from the primary sensory pathways to elicit a conscious sensation had also been observed by Jasper and Bertrand (1966). As already described, stimulus pulses must be

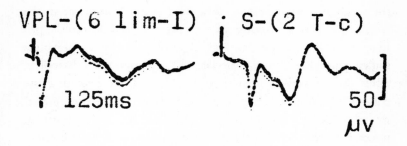

VPL-(6 lim-I) ; S-(2 T-c)

125ms                          50
                               μV

**Fig. 2.5.** Single primary EP responses do *not* elicit any sensation. A train of stimulus pulses to the ascending sensory pathway in the thalamus (the VPL nucleus) does elicit a sensation, just as a train (0.5-sec duration) does at the SI cortex. But single pulses to VPL, even at six times the liminal (threshold) intensity, which is effective with a 0.5-sec train of pulses at 20 per sec, elicit no sensation at all.

The initial 125 msec of the ERP response of the SI cortex is shown for single stimuli applied to VPL and those applied to the skin (S). The initial primary EP response to a VPL stimulus, at six times the liminal I needed for a 0.5-sec train of pulses to produce a threshold sensation, is larger than the initial primary EP cortical response to single-pulse skin stimuli (at two times the threshold strength of single S stimuli). Yet these single VPL stimuli elicit *no* sensation, while these single S stimuli do elicit a moderately strong sensation. The appropriate later components of ERP produced by the single S pulse (not shown in this 125-msec tracing) are not present in the ERP produced by the single VPL stimuli.

Note the delay (after the stimulus artifact) for the primary EP is much shorter for the single VPL stimuli than for the S stimuli. That is because the VPL site is much closer to the SI cortex than is the S stimulus to a hand. From Libet et al., 1967.

applied repetitively here to produce a conscious sensation, just as for stimuli at the sensory cortex.

Because the early primary response of the cortex (to a skin pulse) does not elicit a sensory awareness, some later response components must be required to achieve the awareness. In fact, the single pulse to the skin does elicit later components in the recorded electrical response of the cortex, in addition to the primary evoked response (see Figs. 2.4 and 2.5). When a person is under general anesthesia, the later ERP components disappear, while the primary EP may even be enlarged; but of course the patient does not feel any sensation. Similarly, if the strength of the single skin pulse is lowered to a level at which an awake, normal subject reports feeling nothing, the late ERP components are suddenly absent, but a distinct primary EP response can still be recorded at the sensory cortex (Libet at al., 1967).

It follows then, that the *later* responses of the cerebral cortex, produced after a *single pulse to the skin,* appear to be necessary for producing a conscious sensation. These late responses do go on for more than 0.5 sec—long enough to provide the period of activations needed for the postulated delay in awareness, and this occurs even for a normal sensory stimulus at the skin. However, the actual minimum duration of these later evoked components that are required for conscious sensation has not been established. Nor have possible specific components of the late responses been identified as the specific agents for awareness.

### Retroactive, Backward Effects of a Delayed Second Stimulus

The second line of evidence is based on retroactive, backward effects of a delayed second stimulus, one that follows the initial testing one. Retroactive or backward masking between two peripheral sensory stimuli has long been known. With a visual stimulus consisting of a small weak spot of light, a second stronger larger flash that surrounds the first one can block the subjects' awareness of the first one. The second flash has this effect even if it is delayed by up to 100 msec after the initial weak flash (see, for example, Crawford, 1947).

Retroactive masking has also been reported for electrical stimulation of the skin (Halliday and Mingay, 1961). With a test stimulus at threshold strength on one forearm, a suprathreshold conditioning stimulus on the other forearm raised the threshold for the test stimulus. The conditioning stimulus was effective even when it followed the test stimulus by 100 msec, but not when it followed by 500 msec. This retroactive masking at the 100-msec interval must be mediated in the central nervous system because the test and conditioning stimuli were delivered via different sensory pathways.

What has this backward masking to do with our postulated delay in sensory awareness? If appropriate neural activations must go on in the brain for up to 0.5 sec, to produce awareness, then a second stimulus delivered during that required interval may interfere with the proper completion of those activations and thereby block that sensory awareness. We wanted to establish that such masking takes place in the responding structures at the level of the brain, rather than in a peripheral sensory structure. We also wanted to see whether the time interval between the two stimuli, to produce the retroactive effect, could be increased to something closer to our 0.5-sec requirements.

To achieve these goals, we applied the delayed conditioning stimulus directly to the somatosensory cortex (see Fig. 2.6A). The first (test) stimulus was a weak single pulse to the skin. The delayed cortical stimulus was applied with a large 1-cm disk electrode. It was relatively strong and produced a sensation that was felt in a skin area overlapping the area of sensation produced by the skin pulse. The subjects had no difficulty in distinguishing

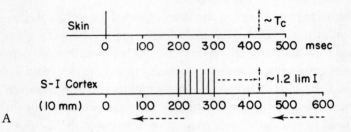

RETROACTIVE MASKING OF S BY C-TRAIN

A

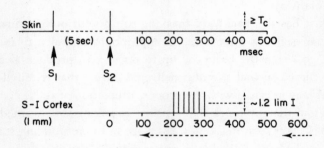

RETROACTIVE ENHANCEMENT OF S BY C-TRAIN

B

**Fig. 2.6.** Retroactive effects of a delayed cortical stimulus that follows a single pulse stimulus to the skin.

A. Retroactive masking of skin sensation. A brief train of electrical pulses is delivered to the primary somatosensory cortex (SI), *beginning* 200 msec (or more) after the weak stimulus pulse (at threshold—T—strength) to the skin. The cortical stimulus electrode is a 1-cm disc, applied to the cortical area that "represents" the skin area being tested.

B. Retroactive enhancement of the subjective sensation, elicited by single pulse stimuli to the skin. The cortical stimulus electrode is a 1-mm contact by a wire.

Top line: Two identical single pulse stimuli to the skin ($S_1$ and $S_2$) are separated by 5 sec. Lower line: A train of stimulus pulses to S-1 cerebral cortex is *begun* at variable times following $S_2$. After each trial, the subject reports whether $S_2$ felt the same as, weaker than, or stronger than $S_1$. From Libet et al., 1992. Reprinted with permission from Elsevier.

the two sensations by their qualities and strengths and by the areas of skin involved.

We did indeed find that the delayed cortical stimulus could mask or block awareness of the skin pulse even when the cortical stimulus began up to 200 to 500 msec after the skin pulse. Incidentally, the delayed cortical stimulus consisted of a train of pulses. Cortical trains lasting less than 100 msec, or single pulses, were *not* effective for this retroactive inhibition.

We also made a surprising discovery that a delayed stimulus could retroactively enhance, or intensify, the initial skin sensation, instead of masking it. This occurred when we used a much smaller electrode contact on the sensory cortex to produce the delayed stimulus. For this experiment, the initial weak skin pulse was delivered twice, the two equal pulses separated by a 5-sec interval (see Fig. 2.6B). The subject was asked to report whether the second of these skin stimuli ($S_2$) felt stronger, the same as, or weaker than the first one ($S_1$). The cortical stimulus was delayed by intervals between 50 msec and 1,000 msec following the second, $S_2$, skin pulse. The subjects reported that $S_2$ felt stronger than $S_1$, in most trials, when the cortical stimulus began, even up to 400 msec or more after $S_2$.

We subsequently found that a retroactive facilitation (or enhancement) had been reported by Pieron and Segal (1939), when the test and conditioning stimuli were both applied via the same electrode on the skin of a finger. The effect was seen when the first or test stimulus was subthreshold. It became perceptible when the suprathreshold conditioning stimulus followed the test stimulus by 20 to 400 msec.

Clearly, then, the conscious sensation elicited by a weak skin pulse could be retroactively modified by a second input that was delayed by about 500 msec. This adequately supported our postulated requirement for about 0.5 sec of cerebral activities to produce awareness of the skin stimulus.

The finding of the *retroactive enhancement* provided an important theoretical element in this support. For retroactive masking/inhibition, some have argued that the delayed cortical stimulus may simply disrupt the formation of the memory for the skin stimulus that preceded it. That argument was in part based on the fact that a generalized strong electrical stimulus to a large area of the brain (as in electroshock therapy) destroys some recent memories. But in such electroconvulsive shock therapy, applied therapeutically to patients with intractable depression, a large portion of the brain is excited strongly, thereby producing a seizure. For our retroactive effects, the delayed stimulus to the sensory cortex was both localized to a small area and set at far below the strength required to elicit even a local seizure in the cortex. The argument for a memory disruption in backward masking is therefore very weak. But, with *retroactive enhancement,* there is no memory loss at all. The subject remembers the second skin stimulus as being stronger than the first control stimulus.

### *Efforts to Deliberately Slow Responses*

The third line of evidence appeared fortuitously in unrelated experiments by Arthur Jensen (1979), a professor of psychology at the University of California–Berkeley campus. Jensen was measuring the reaction times (RT) of different groups of subjects. In these routine tests, subjects were asked to press a button as quickly as possible after the appearance of an agreed-upon signal. With the kinds of signal employed, Jensen's subjects produced RTs in the 200–300 msec range. Because there were differences in the average RTs between different groups of subjects, Jensen wanted to rule out the possibility that some differences

were the result of deliberate lengthening of RTs by some subjects. He therefore had all the subjects repeat their RTs, but
asked them to deliberately lengthen their previous RT by 100
msec or so. To his surprise, he found that none of the subjects
could do that. Instead, they produced RTs of 600–800 msec,
much longer than the requested smaller increases.

When Jensen heard about our evidence for a delay of about
500 msec for conscious sensory awareness, he realized that
might explain his strange finding. To lengthen an RT by a deliberate process, you may assume that the subject must first become aware of the stimulus. Awareness of the stimulus is probably not required at the moment when the subject reacts in the
usual RT test, in which deliberating about the responses is not
an issue. (Indeed, there is direct evidence that ordinary RTs are
accomplished before or with no awareness of the stimulus).
But, to achieve awareness before a deliberate slowing of the response, a requirement of about 500 msec of activities to produce
awareness would delay the response by that additional time.
That would explain the discontinuous jump in RT by an additional 300–600 msec when deliberate slowing of the response is
attempted. This is the only available explanation of Jensen's finding, and it provides additional convincing evidence for a 0.5 sec
delay in sensory awareness.

### How Does the 0.5-Sec
### Neuronal Activity Lead to Awareness?

Is there a unique feature in the brain process that explains why
a 0.5-sec duration of cerebral activations is required to elicit
awareness of an event? Are there testable options for such as
event? There are several possibilities.

First, this time requirement is unique for awareness itself. We have shown that it is possible to accurately detect and respond to a sensory stimulus without any conscious awareness of the stimulus (see Libet et al., 1991). Furthermore, simply to add awareness of the stimulus to that correct detection, we had to increase the duration of repetitive activations of sensory cortex by about 0.4 sec. Clearly, *awareness* itself is a mental phenomenon separate from the content of a mental event. Content of an event can be detected by the brain unconsciously, without awareness of it.

Are special neurons fired after sufficient repetitive actions? Maybe the repeated neuronal activations produce a progressive rise in the excitatory level in some key neurons, so that these neurons finally achieve a firing level. It would then be the discharge of impulses in such special nerve cells that lead to the appearance of awareness. There is some evidence related to this opinion.

Stimuli to the sensory cortex, or to the ascending sensory pathway in the brain, produce no sensory awareness at all if the intensity of the stimulus pulses remains below a liminal (absolute threshold) level. (This level is that required to produce the weakest sensation.) This is true even if the subliminal pulses are repeated for 5 sec or longer. These subliminal pulses do elicit electrical responses of the cortex similar to, but smaller than, those for the effective liminal intensity stimuli. On the other hand, it is possible that the subliminal intensity is not strong enough to ever excite some crucial nerve cell elements, whose repetitive activation leads to the adequate excitatory state in the key neurons for awareness.

With a stimulus in the ascending sensory pathway (medial lemniscus), a single stimulus pulse can be made forty times as strong as each of the pulses in a 0.5-sec train of ten pulses that produces a sensation. Yet that single strong pulse does not elicit any conscious sensation; the subject reports not feeling anything. Instead it is detectable by the subject at an *unconscious* level. That single pulse contains four times the electric charge that the 0.5-sec train delivers at the liminal intensity for a sensation. This tends to contradict the idea that a simple integrative mechanism develops during the 0.5-sec train of pulse that reaches an effective level for awareness. The strong single pulse might be expected to excite all the neurons that would finally be excited by the cumulative integrative effects of the 0.5-sec train of weaker pulses.

A final point can be made against the idea that awareness results from a special firing of some key neurons, at the end of a minimum stimulus train of pulses. This is seen in the recordable electrical responses at the sensory cortex (Fig. 2.7). These responses exhibit no special change at the end, or just after the end, of the required 0.5-sec train. The responses are all essentially identical during that stimulus train. However, one must admit that some special response could have occurred in some nerve cells that was not recordable in our studies.

Robert Doty (my friend and an eminent neuroscientist) has asked, "Is there something about the *frequency* of repetition," rather than duration *per se,* "that is the essential factor?" Or, does attaining conscious experience depend on "the *number* of impulses being generated by the train" of stimulus pulses? The results with different stimulus frequencies do not support these alternative suggestions. Stimulus trains to cortex at 60 pps required a lower liminal intensity than those at 30 pps. But the minimum required train duration was similar for both stimulus frequencies, at their respective liminal intensities. Therefore, neither the higher frequency nor the number of pulses with the 60

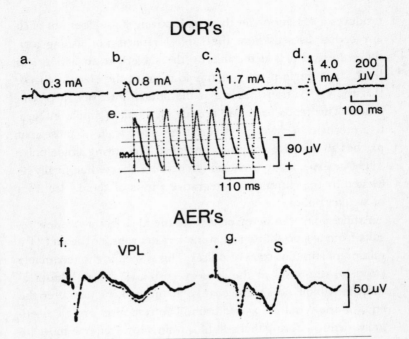

**Fig. 2.7.** Direct cortical responses (DCRs) evoked in SI cortex by adjacent stimulus pulses, at threshold (liminal) strength for conscious sensation.

Upper row: Single responses at different strengths of pulses: a at 0.3 mA; b at 0.8 mA (equal to liminal intensity, for 0.5 sec train of 20 pulses per sec to elicit a sensation); c at 1.7 mA; d at 5 mA. Subject reported not feeling any of these single pulses. Horizontal bar in d is for 100 msec; vertical bar is 200 μV.

Lower row e: 0.5-sec train of responses to 20 per sec pulses at 0.8 mA (same strength as in b in the upper row, but at higher amplification). From Libet, 1973.

pps was significant. It was the duration of train that was critical to elicit awareness.

I have proposed a completely different option for explaining the 0.5-sec activity requirement for awareness: The *durations of similar activations* may itself be the basis. That is, when the duration of repetitive similar activations of appropriate neurons reaches a certain value, then the phenomenon of awareness emerges. The required duration would be the "neuronal code" for the emergence of awareness. This option fits with all the presently available evidence. It is, therefore, a viable option, although it cannot be said to be an adequately proven mechanism.

### Role of Memory Formation

There is still another major issue in this question of what accounts for the 0.5-sec duration of activations for awareness. That is the possible role of memory formation.

We have already noted that the only valid evidence of subjective awareness is an introspective report of awareness by the individual who has the experience of it. Obviously, some short-term memory formation must occur for the subject to recall that awareness and report it. Incidentally, short-term or "working" memory is what accounts for our ability to recall events of information some minutes following the event. The ability to recall a 7- or 11-digit telephone number, after seeing it once, is an example of this type of memory. Without further practice, a person would be likely to forget the number within minutes. Long-term memory involves an additional neuronal process, allowing its effect to persist for days, months, or years.

Some academicians have argued that the 0.5-sec duration of activities required for awareness is simply a reflection of the time it takes to produce the short-term memory trace of the event (see Dennett discussion in Libet, 1993). There are at least two ways in which this memory formulation might operate. In one case, the production of the memory trace would itself be regarded as the "code" for awareness. In the other case, awareness of an event would appear without any significant delay;

but, to be reportable, the short-term memory for that awareness would have to be produced by the 0.5-sec period of activations. There is experimental evidence against either of these options, which I will discuss briefly.

### Explicit Memory and the Hippocampus Structure

Reported observations of human subjects provide a major argument against a role for memory formation in the production of awareness. In both human and nonhuman animals, certain structures within the temporal lobes of the cerebral hemispheres are necessary as mediators for the formation of so-called declarative or explicit memories. These kinds of memories are those that can be consciously recalled and reported. They are distinguished from nondeclarative or implicit memories. Implicit memories are formed without any conscious awareness of the event, and they cannot be consciously recalled and reported. They function largely in the learned acquisition of skills, both mechanical and intellectual.

The hippocampus structure in the temporal lobe is the neuronal component that is necessary for mediating the production of explicit memory. Even if one hippocampus were destroyed, the intact structure on the other side of the brain could carry out the memory process. But if both hippocampal structures were destroyed, the person would suffer a profound loss of the ability to form new explicit memories. Such an individual would have virtually no recallable awareness of events that had just taken place. He could not tell you about an event even immediately after it occurred.

Such losses have resulted due to a pathological lesion in both temporal lobes. More definitively, this bilateral loss happened when a surgical procedure to remove an epileptic focus, in the region of the hippocampus, mistakenly removed the normal hippocampus. At the time the surgical mistake happened it was difficult to determine which side was defective. The patient's good structure was excised, leaving the ineffective pathological structure on the other side. This mistake led to the discovery of the role of the hippocampus structures in explicit memory formation.

Now, the interesting observation, for our present purpose, is the following: An individual with a bilateral loss of the hippocampal structures has virtually no recallable awareness of any event or sensory image that has just happened (although long-term memories formed before the loss are recallable). However, such an individual retains the ability to be aware, both of the immediate present and of himself.

A movie of a patient with this type of loss shows a man who is alert and communicative. He is clearly aware of his surroundings and of the psychologist who is interviewing him. He is even aware of his own inability to remember what just happened, and he complains about that as a significant loss in the quality of his life.

This patient had in fact not lost all memory formation. He was able to sit at a computer and learn to play a game of skill. He was unable to explain how he acquired the skill. The memories for the learned skill were obviously of the implicit type, which do not require the function of the hippocampus structures: A different neural pathway must be involved. But there is no awareness associated with implicit memory. And so, implicit memory cannot be employed as an argument that memory has a role for producing awareness.

There is some question about whether there is formation of a declarative memory that persists for at least 0.5 sec after an event, even with the bilateral loss of the hippocampi. Any such short-lived memory could still be a potential basis for the production of awareness. According to Robert Doty, investigators who studied the patient just described were confident "that the patient could remember things for a minute or so." On the other hand, studies of similar patients employed psychological-cognitive tests that did not demand evidence of a conscious recall (for example, Drachman and Arbit, 1966). It is possible, therefore, that the observed short-term memory was actually evidence for some nondeclarative, implicit memory. In that case, it would not be relevant to the question of the role of memory in the delay of a conscious experience. In any case, Larry Squire, a leading researcher in the field of memory processes, has expressed the opinion that conscious experience is independent of the process of memory formation (personal communication). It would appear, then, that the retention of awareness in people with the severely reduced ability to form new explicit memories indicates that the phenomenon of awareness is *not* a function of a memory process. That fundamental observation contradicts any hypothesis that awareness depends on a formation of a memory.

### Classical Conditioning and Awareness

Clark and Squire (1998) discovered an interesting role for awareness in classical conditioning. In classical conditioning, a conditioning stimulus (CS) is presented just before and during the US (unconditional stimulus). The CS can be a tone that does not produce the response initially; the US can be an air puff to the eye that elicits an eye-blink response. After some trials of this combination, the subject (human or experimental animal) responds with an eye blink to the tone *alone*. That, of course, requires a memory process for the CS-US relationships.

This so-called *simple delay conditioning* is intact even in animals with bilateral hippocampal lesions. In *trace conditioning* the CS is arranged to end about 500 to 1,000 msec before the onset of the US. Animals with bilateral hippocampal lesions fail to acquire trace conditioning. Amnesic patients with damage to hippocampal formations are able to learn standard delay conditioning, but also fail to learn and perform trace conditioning—just as in the experimental animals. Normal human volunteers can, of course, acquire the trace conditioning, but only when they are aware of the stimuli. So, trace conditioning not only depends on the hippocampal structures, but it is also somehow coupled to the process for awareness.

Now, these findings do not prove that production of a declarative memory is the basis for the roughly 0.5-sec duration of cerebral activities needed to elicit awareness of an event. Clark and Squire (1998) suggest that

> [a] conjoint operation of the hippocampal system and the neocortex may be a critical element that confers awareness about the (declarative) knowledge that has been acquired. . . . But that does not mean that awareness, *per se,* requires the memory function of the hippocampus. Indeed, the existence of awareness in the absence of declarative knowledge, in patients with bilateral loss of hippocampal systems, supports the view that formation of a declarative memory is a separate process from the unique process for producing awareness itself. The finding that trace conditioning requires subjects to

become *aware* of the temporal relationships among the stimuli explains why trace conditioning is declarative and hippocampus dependent, and it brings classical conditioning, the best studied of all learning paradigms, into register with current understanding of the memory systems of the brain.

An important implication of this finding is that trace conditioning may offer a possible method for studying awareness in nonhuman animals. Simple delay conditioning is nondeclarative; its formation does not require the hippocampus or awareness. It is exhibited by amnesic patients who lack short-term declarative memory.

### Other Evidence on Proposals of Memory for Awareness

Even though the foregoing evidence appears to rule out memory formation to explain the 0.5-sec activities required for awareness, it is interesting and instructive to analyze at least one such proposal. After my lecture in a symposium on consciousness, sponsored by the Ciba Foundation (in London), the philosopher Daniel Dennett proposed that the conscious awareness for an event might appear almost immediately, as it does in fact seem to do for a stimulus at the skin. But, he argued, the awareness cannot be *recalled and reported* unless there is a sufficient duration of neuronal activity to produce and "fixate" the memory for that awareness. Dennett's argument was also intended to exclude the need for postulating a backward referral of the subjective timing of a sensory awareness, as discussed below (see discussion in Libet, 1993b, pp. 140 and onward). At the time, I did not recall the evidence I have already cited: Declarative, explicit memory is not necessary for awareness, and both memory and awareness depend on independent processes. However, I did make other experimental arguments against Dennett's proposed hypothesis.

As I have already noted in the second section of this chapter, it is possible to inhibit or mask the appearance of a conscious sensory experience, if a weak sensory stimulus is followed by a train of stimulus pulses applied to the sensory cortex. This retroactive masking occurs even when that train does not begin until up to 500 msec after the skin pulse. That result demonstrates that a delayed input can interfere with the content of the sensory experiences. I cited that data as evidence that a neuronal activity period is required to produce the sensory awareness.

Dennett countered that the delayed masking stimulus was simply disrupting the formation of the memory trace for the awareness. (Electroconvulsive shock therapy is indeed known to disrupt recent memory formations. However, the delayed masking stimulus employed in our experiments is minuscule in comparison to the strong generalized electric shock used in shock therapy.) But his argument is countered by two other experimental observations: (1) A second masking stimulus can be applied after the first masking stimulus (Dember and Purcell, 1967). The second masker wiped out the sensations for the first masking stimulus, and the awareness for the original skin stimulus then reappeared. That means the first masking stimulus did *not* wipe out the memory trace for the original skin stimulus. (2) When the delayed cortical stimulus is applied by a much smaller electrode contact, the original skin pulse is not masked but actually felt to be stronger (Libet et al., 1992). With this retroactive enhancement of the sensory awareness for a skin stimulus, there was clearly no loss of memory at all.

So, the retroactive effects of a delayed stimulus on the sensation of an original skin pulse do not involve a loss of memory for that skin pulse. Instead, the retroactive effects of a delayed stimulus appear to *modulate* the sensory awareness that develops for the original skin pulse (during the 0.5-sec delay).

Max Velmans also made an ingenious argument against Dennett's proposal (see discussion in Libet, 1993b, pp. 145–146). As Velmans pointed out, Dennett's proposal that sensation may be experienced early but then forgotten is not experimentally falsifiable. For example, in a standard psychophysical procedure, you can establish the threshold for awareness of a sensory stimulus. As you gradually turn up the intensity of the stimulus, a certain point is recorded at which the subject says she can just feel it (or see it, or hear it). Then you can lower the intensity until the subject says she does not feel it. The subject's reports are correlated with the strength of the stimulus and are accepted as accurate and valid. But, according to Dennett's proposal, the subject's inability to report feeling the weaker, below-threshold stimulus could result from rapid forgetting of an actually experienced event. "Dennett could extend that claim to any reports that subjects make about *not* having experienced something." Dennett's view, in other words, could never be contradicted if he would not accept a subject's report of no sensory experience. Such proposals are not scientifically acceptable because they are speculative, untestable beliefs.

I conclude, then, that awareness is a unique phenomenon, with its separate neuronal requirements. Awareness is not a function of a memory process. It is not the equivalent of a formed, declarative memory trace. Nor is the absence of a report of awareness due to a rapid forgetting of an early actual sensory experience. The proposal that remains most compatible with all the evidence is the hypothesis that awareness is the emergent result of appropriate neuronal activities when these persist for a minimum duration, of up to 0.5 sec.

### What Does the Primary Evoked
### Cortical Response to a Sensory Stimulus Do?

You may ask, if the cortical activities that produce the recorded primary EP appear to have no essential role in begetting a sensory awareness, what function does the primary EP serve? The primary neural response is important for the discrimination of the precise location of a stimulus at the skin. And, as we discovered, it appears to provide a timing signal to which the correct *subjective* timing of the input to the skin is retroactively referred. In some forms of a cerebral stroke, there is major damage to this fast, specific sensory pathway as it approaches the sensory cortex. These stroke patients can locate a skin stimulus only in a very crude way, and they lose the ability to tell there are two points of a two-pointed stimulus to a hand until these stimulus points are separated by many centimeters.

In addition to this spatial deficiency, we found, in the one such patient available to us, that a touch pulse at the skin was perceived as delayed by about 0.5 sec, compared to a pulse applied to the normal side (see Libet et al., 1979). This patient had a stroke some years earlier, confined to an area of the right hemisphere. This stroke left her with permanent damage to the specific ascending sensory pathway for bodily sensations. She showed an inability to accurately localize a stimulus to the left hand or arm, and could only report its location very crudely. We tested this patient for her subjective timings of stimuli to the good right hand compared to the deficient left hand. With a small stimulating electrode on the back of each hand, she was given a stimulus to each hand at a strength she could barely feel.

When stimuli were applied simultaneously to both hands, this subject reported that she felt the right hand stimulus before the (bad) left hand one. The stimulus to the affected side had to be delivered about 0.5 sec *prior* to the stimulus to the normal side, in order for the patient to report that both stimuli were felt consciously as being simultaneous. Clearly, she had lost the ability to subjectively refer her sensation in the left hand backward in time. That sensation was therefore subjectively timed with the roughly 500-msec delay imposed by the cerebral requirement for awareness. That loss in the ability to antedate the awareness was presumably due to her loss of the primary evoked response for her left hand.

***Conscious synchronicity of sensations.*** This brings up an important general question about how different stimuli that are actually delivered synchronously can be consciously perceived as being synchronous. With stimuli in the same somatosensory modality, there are different conduction times in the sensory pathways, depending on the different distances between the stimulus locations on the body. The time for the arrival of the fastest sensory messages varies between 5–10 msec (for stimuli at the head) to 30–40 msec (for stimuli to the feet). Because synchronous stimuli to these two areas are subjectively perceived as synchronous, we can only assume that a time difference of 30 msec or so is not subjectively meaningful. On the other hand, a very strong stimulus to one site may require a significantly shorter duration of appropriate cerebral activities; the difference can be as much as 100 to 200 msec for the two different strengths of stimuli. I do not know whether relative subjective timings for two such stimuli have been studied. Perhaps they are not felt as being synchronous. Stimuli sufficiently strong to require significantly shorter cerebral activation times may not occur commonly.

What about synchronously applied stimuli in different modalities? Suppose that a flash of light appears at the same time as a crack of noise, both from the firing of a gun. Of course light travels faster than sound; but if the gun is fired just a few feet away, the difference in travel times would not be significant. (At a speed of about 1,100 feet per second, the sound would reach the listener in about 2 msec from 2 feet away). As with somatosensory stimuli to the body, the visual and the auditory stimuli also elicit a fast primary evoked potential in the visual and auditory cortex respectively. The latency or delay for arrival of the fast signal to the visual cortex is distinctly longer than for the other modalities. That is because the retina takes extra time to get from the photoreceptors through the next neural layer in order to fire the ganglion cells, which send impulses via the optic nerve fibers toward the thalamus and on to the visual cortex. The delays for the visual primary evoked response in the human brain have been measured at about 30 to 40 msec by Goff et al. (1977).

The primary evoked responses at all sensory cortex areas is localized to a small area that represents the peripheral sensory spot or area being stimulated. With a recording electrode on the surface of the cortex, a substantial primary evoked potential will only be recorded at the "hot spot," the spot of cortex receiving the fast input from the peripheral sensory elements that respond to the sensory stimulus. The primary evoked potential is usually not significantly seen in recordings made with an electrode on the scalp because not only may the electrode not be over the hot spot but also the electrical potential produced by the local cortical area is greatly reduced, attenuated by being "short-circuited" in the tissues between the cortex and the scalp. Consequently, the earliest significant electrical potential seen in a scalp recording is a later component of the response to a stimulus. This has a latency of 50–100 msec longer than the time primary evoked potential, and it would be misleading to use the later timing in a consideration of the problem of synchrony among different simultaneous stimuli.

In any case, the true primary evoked potentials can have latencies between about 5 and 40 msec, depending on the location and modality of the stimulus. If all simultaneous stimuli are perceived subjectively as being synchronous, we would have to assume that the brain does not "consider" this range of variability in latencies as subjectively significant.

## Why Get Excited about the Delay in Sensory Awareness?

If we look at some of the ramifications of our findings for a delay in sensory awareness, the implications are quite astounding. We consider a larger variety of important implications later in this section, but I mention a few obvious ones here.

First, if awareness of all sensory stimuli is delayed by about 0.5 sec, following the pattern found for somatic sensations, then our *awareness of our sensory world is substantially delayed* from its actual occurrence. What we become aware of has already happened about 0.5 sec earlier. We are not conscious of the actual moment of the present. We are always a little late. If that is so, how can one explain the fact that subjectively we feel that we are aware at the actual moment of a sensory event? I consider that question at length in the next section.

Second, it is well established that the image reported by a subject may be considerably different from the actual image shown to the subject. For example, if a prudish man were shown a picture of a naked lady, he might report seeing something quite different, or he might report that he saw no image. The subject would not be consciously and deliberately distorting the report; instead, he would appear to believe that he was giving a report of what he saw. That is, the distortion of the content appears to take place unconsciously. Sigmund Freud was, of course, one of the first to call attention to what he postulated was a suppression of conscious content. That suppression would be brought about by unconscious processes that "protect" the subject from an unpleasant conscious experience.

Given such unconscious modification of what we become aware, there must clearly be some delay in the awareness during which such a subjective modulation can be produced. If awareness of a sensory image were produced almost immediately, with no substantial delay, it would be very difficult to imagine how an unconscious cerebral process could then be mobilized to produce a modified content of that awareness without the subject knowing it.

Our discovery of the substantial cerebral delay for awareness thus provides a physiologically required time interval during which other inputs may modulate the content of an experience before it consciously appears. As previously described, the retroactive effects of a delayed cortical stimulus can, in fact, subconsciously change the conscious content of a skin sensation, as reported by the subjects in our experiments.

There are many philosophical meanings that we could derive from the existence of a delay (of up to 0.5 sec) in conscious awareness, after the actual time at which events occur. We would have to modify the existentialist view of living in the experience of the "now"; our experience of the "now" is always delayed or late.

Further, there is the possibility provided for each person's character or past experience to alter the conscious content of each event. That means each person has his or her own individual conscious reality. The 0.5-sec delay for awareness of an event makes that possible. Differing perceptions of reality may have meaning for the different paths that people follow, based on each individual's conscious perceptions of reality.

In any case, our knowledge of a substantial delay for awareness shakes up our confidence in our certainties about realities of the world.

### Antedating of Delayed Sensory Experience

The evidence appears to show that some appropriate neuronal activities in the brain must endure for up to about 500 msec for even a single-pulse skin stimulus, in order to elicit a conscious sensory experience. But subjectively we seem to be aware of a skin stimulus almost immediately, with no appreciable delay. So we have a strange paradox: Neural activity requirements in the brain indicate that the experience or awareness of a skin stimulus cannot appear until after some 500 msec, yet subjectively we believe it was experienced without such a delay.

This troublesome dilemma bothered us for some time, until I began to think that *subjective* timing need not be identical to *neuronal* time (in other words, the time when the neurons ac-

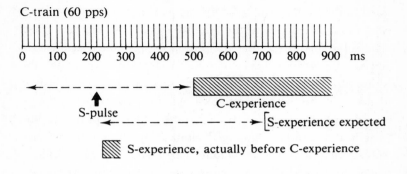

C-train (60 pps)

0   100   200   300   400   500   600   700   800   900   ms

S-pulse

C-experience

[S-experience expected

S-experience, actually before C-experience

**Fig. 2.8.** Subjective timing of sensory experience with cerebral versus skin stimuli.

Cortical stimulus train at 60 pulses per sec, at liminal intensity for threshold sensory experience. Because the train must last 500 msec, the sensation it produces cannot begin before the 500-msec time period. A single threshold pulse to skin (S) is applied at the 200-msec duration of that cortical train. If that also required 500 msec to be developed, the S sensation should be felt *after* the C-induced sensation. But subject reports the S sensation felt before the C-induced sensation. That held true when the S pulse was further delayed. But when the S pulse was applied near the 500-msec time of the cortical train, the subject reported both sensations were felt at the same time. From Libet et al., 1979. Reprinted with permission from Oxford University Press and *Brain*, vol. 102, pp. 191–222.

tually produced the experience). Indeed, we ran an experiment that demonstrated this discrepancy directly (Fig. 2.8; Libet et al., 1979). For this test, the train of stimulus pulses (near-threshold strength for awareness) was applied to the sensory cortex and required about the usual 500 msec of repetition to produce a conscious sensory experience. (This cortically induced sensation was reported to appear in an area of skin like the hand. It was not felt to appear in the brain.) We then added a single, near-threshold pulse to the skin. This pulse was applied at different times after the start of the cortical train, in different trials. After each trial with the coupled cortical and skin stimuli, the subject was asked to tell us which of the two sensations appeared first. The subject reported that the sensations generated at the skin appeared *before* the cortically induced sensation, even when the skin pulse was delayed by some hundreds of milliseconds after the start of the cortical stimulus. It was only when the skin pulse was delayed by about 500 msec that the subjects reported feeling that both sensations appeared almost simultaneously. Clearly, subjective time of the skin-induced experience appeared to have no delay, relative to that for the cortically induced experience. The cortically induced sensation was delayed by about 500 msec relative to the skin-induced sensation.

We already had good evidence that awareness of a skin pulse does require about 500 msec of activities in the brain, similar to that found with a cortical stimulus. Yet the skin pulse appeared to be timed subjectively as if there were no such substantial delay. How could we deal with this paradoxical empirical dilemma? Is there a mechanism in the brain that could account for the discrepancy?

The clue to a possible answer came from the difference between the electrical response of the cortex to a skin stimulus versus to a cortical-surface stimulus. The skin pulse elicits a characteristic response of the sensory cortex that begins with a wave or component about 10–30 msec after the skin stimulus. This is the primary EP, which is followed by later EP waves or components. However, the stimulus pulses applied to the surface of the sensory cortex do not elicit any response that resembles the primary EP (at least not with cortical stimuli in the range of intensity we used).

This difference in cortical EP responses to the two different sites of stimulus (skin versus cortical surface) led me to propose a unique hypothesis to explain the paradoxical timings. In this hypothesis (see Fig. 2.8) the awareness of the skin stimulus is in fact delayed in its appearance until the end of the roughly 500 msec of appropriate brain activities. But then, there is a *subjective referral of the timing* for that experience *back to the time of the primary EP response!* The primary EP response of the cortex begins only about 10–30 msec after the skin stimulus, depending on how far the stimulated skin is from the brain. This delay of 10–30 msec is not sufficient to be experienced consciously. The experience or awareness of the skin pulse would thus be antedated (referred backward in time) subjectively to the timing signal provided by the primary EP response. The skin-induced sensation appears subjectively as if there were no delay, even though it did not actually appear until after the 500 msec required for neuronal adequacy to elicit that sensory experience.

This rather outrageous hypothesis could not be seriously proposed without an experimental test of its validity. (An experimental test, or at least its design, is mandatory for any scientific hypothesis.). Fortunately, we were able to devise an adequate, crucially effective experimental test.

The test was based on the interesting fact that stimuli in the specific ascending sensory pathway in the brain (in other words, in the medial lemniscus bundle; see Fig. 2.3), have two relevant features. First, to elicit a conscious sensation, stimuli require durations up to about 500 msec, just as for stimuli at the sensory cortex. Second, *each* individual stimulus pulse in a 500-msec train of pulses in the medial lemniscus elicits a fast primary EP response recordable at the sensory cortex. This is the same as the response of the sensory cortex to a skin stimulus. It is unlike the stimuli at the surface of the sensory cortex, which do not produce any such primary EP.

According to our hypothesis for backward referral of subjective timing, the generation of the putative timing signal (primary EP response) by even the first stimulus pulse of the pulse train in medial lemniscus should make the subjective reported timing of sensory awareness the same as that for a skin pulse (Fig. 2.9). So in the experimental test, we matched a suitable train of stimulus pulses to medial lemniscus with a single effective pulse to skin. This experiment was similar in design to that discussed earlier, when a skin pulse was matched with a train of pulses delivered to the brain's sensory cortex. The subject was asked to report which of these two sensations appeared (subjectively) first, in other words, the sensation elicited by the medial lemniscus versus the sensation elicited by the skin pulse.

The results of that experiment, to our delighted surprise, confirmed the prediction from our hypothesis. When the skin pulse was delivered at the same time as the start of the medial lemniscus train, subjects tended to report that both sensations appeared at the same time. But we knew that the subjects could not possibly have experienced the medial lemniscus sensation until the required 500 msec (or 200 msec with stronger stimuli) had gone by. They felt nothing if the train of pulses to medial lemniscus were cut to less than the required duration of 500 msec. As in the case of medial lemniscus, the skin pulse sensation was reported to appear before that from the cortical stimulus. Only when the skin pulse was delayed until the end of the required cortical train were the two sensations reported to appear at the same time.

So, we see that even though both the cortical and the medial lemniscus stimuli required similar durations of repetitive pulses to produce the sensory experience, the subjective timing of the

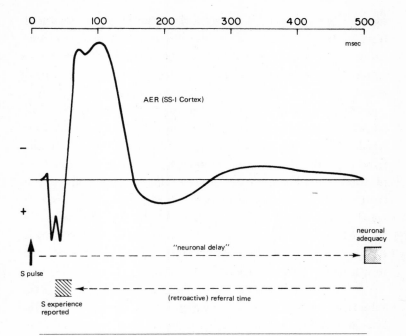

**Fig. 2.9.** Diagram of hypothesis for subjective referral of a sensory experience backward in time (antedating of experience).

The average evoked response (AER) was recorded at the SI cerebral cortex in response to single pulses, just above threshold for sensation, applied (at the S pulse arrow) to the skin of the hand centralateral to this recording site.

The first dashed line below the AER shows the delay to achieve "neuronal adequacy" for producing the sensation (based on other evidence). The second dashed line shows the putative subjective referral of the sensory experience back to the time of the initial primary evoked potential in the AER. This accounted for the observation that the subject reports the time of the experience as showing no significant delay after the stimulus to the skin. From Libet et al., 1979. Reprinted with permission from Oxford University Press and *Brain*, vol. 102, pp. 191–222.

experience was reported to be much earlier for the medial lemniscus stimulus. As noted, the two stimuli differed in the electrical responses of the sensory cortex. Only the medial lemniscus stimulus elicited a primary EP response to each of its pulses. It shares that effect with the single pulse to the skin.

Some have raised a criticism that the test is based on the "unnatural" nature of the medial lemniscus stimulation. We can brush that aside by simply comparing the results when a medial lemniscus stimulus is matched against a cortical stimulus. Both of these stimulus sites are "unnatural," but any difference in their behavior is clearly meaningful. Because the minimum neuronal delays for the experience were similar for both cases, the earlier subjective timing for the medial lemniscus stimuli must be taken as direct evidence for backward referral of its subjective timing of the sensory experience.

We have, then, produced strong and direct evidence that the subjective timing of a sensory experience is antedated from the later minimum time at which the brain activities actually become adequate to produce the experience. The subjective timing is referred backward to a "timing signal": the primary EP response of the sensory cortex. That accounts for our subjective feeling and belief that we become aware of a sensory signal virtually immediately, even though there is in fact a substantial delay!

This subjective referral backward in time, of our conscious sensory awareness, also accounts for another phenomenon: We may ask, what happens to subjective timings of different skin sensory stimuli, which are different in strengths and locations, but are all delivered at the same time? Subjectively, we feel or believe that all these stimuli were applied synchronously. This issue is discussed earlier, in the section "What Does the Primary Evoked Cortical Response to a Sensory Stimulus Do?"

### Subjective Referral of Experiences

We have just seen, in the previous section, that the subjective timing of a sensory experience may not correspond with the delayed time at which the cerebral neurons actually elicit that experience. The sensory experience is automatically and unconsciously subjectively referred backward to the time of the first, fast cortical response to the sensory signal.

An analogous situation was already known for the spatial image of a sensory event. The sensory image that one becomes aware of subjectively looks very different from the spatial pattern of neuron activities that elicited that image.

The most obvious and direct illustration of subjective referrals, being felt at different locations from the site of actual stimulus, can be seen when you directly stimulate the cerebral somatosensory cortex. The subject does not feel or experience the resulting sensation as located in the brain, where it was produced. Rather, the subject feels the sensation to be located in a place in the body that is normally related to that spot in the brain. For example, if a certain cortical spot is stimulated, the subject feels that her hand has been stimulated. She subjectively refers the spatial location out from the brain to some bodily structure. She is completely unaware of the activity in the stimulated area of the sensory cortex.

Descartes theorized in the seventeenth century that the experience of a sensation occurred only when the appropriate area of the brain was excited, but that the subjective location of the sensation was experienced to be at the normal sites of sensory input. He proposed that this was true even when the sensory system is excited anywhere in the central nervous system! That proposal is amazingly similar to the present direct evidence supporting this view.

A related sort of subjective referral occurs in the spatial locations for all normal sensory inputs. Take a visual image: The light pattern from the visible object activates a pattern of optic nerve impulses that reach the visual cortex after transmittal through some relay stations. The spatial arrangement of the cortical nerve cells that respond to the optical input appears in a very distorted pattern, compared to the actual image presented to the eye. In fact, the original visual object would not be recognizable from a map of the cortical responses to its lighted input. The cortical response may be greatly distorted spatially when compared to the image that we *subjectively see*. But, in fact, it is the spatially distorted cortical representation that gives rise to the image you experience. We must therefore conclude that the brain's distorted neural pattern, in response to a visual image, is *subjectively* referred or projected into space, in such a way that the image seen corresponds better and more accurately to the actual visual object.

We have now established experimentally that there is also subjective referral of the *timing* of a sensory experience. This is in a way analogous to spatial referral. Although stimulation, in the cerebral sensory pathway to the cortex, may have to go on for up to 0.5 sec to elicit a conscious sensation, subjects report that subjectively the sensation appears without any significant delay. The delayed experience is subjectively referred back in time to the timing signal provided by the fast primary EP response of the sensory cortex. Subjects unconsciously and automatically refer the timing of the sensory event back to the time of the initial fast response of the sensory cortex. They are not aware that the sensory experience *did not actually begin* until adequate cerebral stimulation of up to 0.5 sec in duration had taken place.

### *Subjective Referrals "Correct" the Neural Representation*

Subjective referrals of the spatial and temporal features of a sensory event have the effect of subjectively correcting the neuronal distortions of the sensory event. The distortions are imposed by the way in which the cerebral neurons represent the event, both in space and in time. So, in our conscious experience of a sensory event, the event seems to occur when it actually happened, instead of 0.5 sec. later (when we, in fact, became aware of the event). It is of further interest that the specific projection pathway to the sensory cortex provides the signal used by both the spatial and the temporal referrals. Damage to this pathway, as in some cerebral strokes, results in losses both in subjective localizations of a stimulus and in subjective timings of the stimulus.

An *unconscious* ability to localize stimuli is available. In the phenomenon of blindsight, subjects can localize targets by correctly pointing at an image, even though a lesion of the primary visual area has destroyed the specific primary projection system and the subjects do not consciously see the targets. It appears that the specific sensory projection to the primary visual area is required only for *subjective* localization, not for unconscious localization.

The subjective "corrections" of the information supplied by the sensory cortex are apparently learned. The most direct evidence that subjective referrals are learnable phenomena comes from some amazing experiments reported some years ago. Human subjects were fitted with prism spectacles that turned the visual image upside down (Stratton, 1897; Snyder and Pronko, 1952). At first, the subjects did see the world upside down. Also, the subjects could not point accurately to a spot in the visual field.

However, after wearing these spectacles continuously for about a week, subjects began to be able to behave as if the image were normal. A subject replying to a question about his subjective experience reported that he was not aware of the inverted visual image; but, when asked, he recalled it actually did look upside down! Objectively, of course, the visual input was still reversed from its normal arrangement. In other words, this subject somehow learned to not pay attention to the inversion and adapted his visuomotor responses as if the image were upright. When the spectacles were removed, the subject's visuomotor accuracy was again briefly less accurate; it recovered within a few days. The experiment indicated that the adapted behavioral change was not due to an actual subjective inversion of the image; rather, the awareness of the upside-down image was somehow suppressed.

Interestingly, such flexibility of the visuomotor referral mechanism is not seen in all animals. When Roger Sperry (1950) turned the eyes of frogs around, so the eyes were "upside down," the frogs always reached into the upside-down visual fields seen by those eyes. They did not learn to respond to the inverted image correctly.

These characteristics of visuomotor referral suggest that newborn infants may have difficulties with their still-not-adaptively-organized visual images. They may need to learn to behaviorally refer the visual information in a way that produces an image that corresponds to the real sensory image. Perhaps infants initially see a distorted image that corresponds to the distorted representation of the sensory input on the visual cortex! Perhaps the time required to learn to refer this distorted representation to a "corrected" image may help explain why infants seem not to see properly until about a month or so after birth. Can the vision experts devise a way to test such a hypothesis?

Then there is the interesting question of how each primary sensory area of the cerebral cortex elicits its own specific quality of a subjective sensation, when activated by a proper electrical stimulus or by the arrival of its normal sensory input. That is, stimulation of the somatosensory cortex in the postcentral gyrus elicits subjective bodily sensations (touch, pressure, motion, warm, cold, though not pain). Stimulation of the visual cortex (striate cortex in the occipital pole at the rear) elicits visual sensations. Stimulation of the auditory cortex (upper lip of the temporal lobe) elicits sensations of sounds. Although there is some difference in the arrangement of the neurons in these different areas, the basic neuronal structures and their synaptic interconnections are similar. Stimulation of most other areas of the cerebral cortex does not elicit any conscious experience. That is not because the nerve cells are unresponsive to stimulation in these nonsensory areas. It is presumably due to the inability of the electrically excited nerve fibers to activate a more complex network of nerve cells that serve the functions of the nonsensory areas.

Well, each sensory input becomes able to produce the specific subjective quality of sensation normally produced in each case. A question then arises as to whether the same specific sensation would be elicited if the sensory input to the area were changed. That question has led some scientists to pose a strange question: What would happen if we led the acoustic sensory pathway into a functional connection with the visual area of cortex, and led the visual sensory pathway into making a functional connection with the hearing area of the cortex? Would we then see the thunder and hear the lightning? This kind of experiment cannot, of course, be carried out on human subjects. But it has been, in a limited way, carried out in ferrets (Sharma et al., 2000); Melchner et al., 2000).

In the neonatal ferret, the ascending retinal pathway was rerouted into the MGN (medial geniculate nucleus). (This nucleus normally receives the ascending auditory pathway and then projects its axons to the auditory cortex in the temporal lobe.) The normally ascending auditory pathway to the MGN was cut below the MGN. The animals were then raised to adulthood before testing. The researchers found neurons, in the normally auditory cortex, that responded to *visual* stimuli. These "rewired" neurons were organized into orientation modules, comparable to normally innervated visual cortex. In addition, the ferrets responded to light stimuli (presented in the portion of visual field "seen" only by the altered projection) as though they perceived the stimuli to be visual rather than auditory. So the perceptual modality of a primary sensory cortex is affected by the input it receives. Of course, the ferrets could not tell the researchers what they subjectively perceived.

### General Implications of Subjective Referrals

Subjective referrals of cerebral *sensory* responses, spatially and temporally, depend on the availability of the fast and localized primary responses of sensory cortex. In the absence of these primary responses, the subjective referrals become inadequate or completely absent. But perhaps there is another sense in which all subjective experiences are "referred." Subjective experiences of mental events, generally, are not reducible to or describable by the activities of the nerve cells that give rise to the experiences. As noted in Chapter 1, a complete knowledge of the neuron activities would tell you nothing about the subjective experiences they may elicit. To get at the latter, you must ask for an introspective report of the experience by the individual, who alone has "access" to his conscious functions. Put it another way: The nature and content of a conscious experience do not "look like" the pattern of nerve cell activities that produces that experience. You might therefore propose that the nature and content of all subjective experiences are referred into the mental sphere, from the nerve cell patterns of activity that seem to elicit the experiences.

### Neural Mechanisms for Subjective Referrals?

There is another aspect of subjective referrals that may be of fundamental importance to the nature of the mind-brain relationship. There appears to be no *neural mechanism* that could be viewed as directly mediating or accounting for the referrals!

Take the case of how the primary evoked potential can act as the cortical response to which the subjective spatial location and the subjective timing of a sensory stimulus are referred. How does that happen? This primary EP appears even when a sensory stimulus is below the threshold for sensation. It then appears alone, without any later evoked EPs. The later components, EPs lasting 0.5 sec or more, appear when the stimulus strength equals and exceeds the threshold for sensation (see Libet et al., 1967). The primary EP is exhibited only in a highly localized small area of sensory cortex. But the later EPs are not confined to the primary sensory cortex; related responses are broadly distributed in the cortex. A broad spread of activities with a single visual event, presumably one above threshold, has been described by others (see Buchner et al., 1997).

It is the primary EP response alone that appears to provide

the signal to which subjective awareness of the timing and spatial localization is referred. It becomes difficult, then, to describe an additional neural process that could mediate this retroactive referral of a delayed sensory experience back to the primary EP response, although such a mechanism is not impossible. If the primary EP response is the timing agent without the mediation by other unknown neural actions, it would appear that subjective referrals are purely a mental function, with no corresponding neural basis in the brain.

But the issue of mental functions related to neural ones is far broader than the specific one of subjective referrals of conscious sensory experiences. All the brain processes that give rise to subjective conscious experiences (including thoughts, intentions, self-awareness, and so on) do not "look like" the emergent experiences. Indeed, even a complete knowledge of the responsible neural processes would not, *a priori,* describe the accompanying mental events. (The two phenomena have to be studied together to discover correlations.) The transformation from neuronal patterns to a subjective representation would appear to develop in the mental sphere that has emerged from that neuronal pattern. (The use of some specific neural signals to guide the sensory referrals does not tell us how the referral is achieved.)

How does the inference of *no* direct neural description of subjective sensory referral and other mental events relate to certain philosophical views of the mind-brain relationship? First, such a proposal does *not* invoke or constitute an instance of dualism, in a Cartesian sense. That is, the proposal does not entail a separable or independent existence for the physical brain and the mental phenomena. My view of mental subjective function is that it is an emergent property of appropriate brain functions. The conscious mental cannot exist without the brain processes that give rise to it. However, having emerged from brain activities as a unique "property" of that physical system, the mental can exhibit phenomena not evident in the neural brain that produced it. This view follows that espoused by Roger Sperry on emergent properties of a system (for more detail, see Chapters 5 and 6).

Identity theory is probably the most commonly held philosophical theory for relating the "physical" to the "mental" (see Hook, 1960). In a simplified version of identity theory, the externally observable features of the brain's structure and function— in other words, the physically observable aspects—describe the external or outer quality of the system. The mental events, conscious or unconscious, describe an "inner quality" of the *same system* or "substrate." That is, the given substrate is responsible for both the outer and inner qualities described. Identity theory recognizes that subjective experiences are accessible only (as an inner quality) to the individual who has them. But, if there is no specific neural (physical event) that corresponds to a mental event (like subjective referrals in space and time), then there is no common substrate to provide the identity for these outer and inner qualities. One of the early leaders for identity theory was the late Stephen Pepper (1960), Professor of Philosophy at the University of California–Berkeley. In my discussions with Professor Pepper, he promptly realized that our findings of subjective referral backward in time would create serious difficulties for identity theory. That is particularly true if there is no neural counterpart for this mental operation.

Identity theorists may say that this apparent disconnection between observable and inner (mental) qualities is simply the way the two aspects (the outer and inner) of their common single substrate are expressed. But that would seem to gloss over difficulties by applying a word, the common substrate, to cover all the properties. Besides, the so-called substrate is a speculative construction that cannot be falsified by any test. In any case, it is clear that inner, mental phenomena have features quite different from those of the physically observable brain, and that the inner and outer qualities are each not describable, *a priori*, in terms of the other.

A separate issue is how to regard one's view or experience of the present, the "now." The delay, of up to 0.5 sec, in the appearance of awareness of a sensory event introduced a difficulty in how to define or understand "the present moment." However, existence of subjective referral backward in time (to the time of the fast primary response of sensory cortex) does put the *subjective experience* of the present back into the present. So we have the strange situation in which actual awareness of the present is really delayed, but the *content* of the conscious *experience* is brought into alignment with the present. Subjectively, then, we do live in the antedated present, although in fact we are not aware of the present for up to 0.5 sec after the sensory signal arrives at the cerebral cortex.

These implications have serious consequences for certain views of the present. For example, Ludwig Wittgenstein is reported to have stated: "The present is neither past or future. To experience the present is therefore a phenomenon with timelessness." But if our experience of a sensory stimulus is actually antedated after the 0.5-sec delay, the experience is actually one of an event 0.5 sec in the past. And so, the subjective "present" is actually of a sensory event in the past; it is not "timeless."

Endogenous conscious events (our thoughts, imaginations, nonsensory feelings, and so on) differ from normal sensory experience. Referral backward in time, the antedating of a sensory experience, only is known to happen when the primary cortical response elicited by the fast sensory input is available to act as a training signal for the referral. Endogenous, nonsensory conscious events do not have such a timing signal available. If the endogenous conscious events also require up to 0.5 sec of appropriate neural activations to produce awareness—in other words, if they follow our putative principle of this requirement for all awareness—then the endogenous conscious events would all be experienced after a delay. The delay would be from the beginning of the unconscious neural events postulated to initiate all awarenesses.

# 3

## UNCONSCIOUS AND CONSCIOUS MENTAL FUNCTIONS

You are driving along in your car at 30 mph on a city street. Suddenly, a young boy steps into the street in front of your car, chasing a ball. You slam your foot on the brake pedal to bring the car to a screeching halt. Were you consciously aware of the event before stepping on the brake? Or was that an unconscious action that you became aware of after you hit the brakes?

### Unconscious Mental Functions

Our experimental evidence, described in Chapter 2, showed that activations of the sensory cortex have to proceed for up to about 500 msec to produce awareness of a sensory signal. When the duration of the liminal stimulus to the sensory cortex was reduced below that threshold—such as to 400 msec or even 450 msec—no sensory awareness was reported. The subjects reported, "I felt nothing." A similar situation was found for trains of stimulus pulses applied to the specific ascending sensory pathway in the brain; this is the fast pathway from the medulla to cerebral cortex.

In spite of this presumed actual delay in the awareness of the

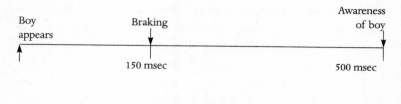

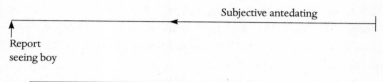

**Fig. 3.1.** Sequence of events when a boy steps in front of a moving car.

boy and the ball for up to 500 msec, you are capable of slamming on the brake in about 150 msec or less after the boy appeared (see Fig. 3.1). That action, therefore, must be performed unconsciously, without awareness. Amazingly, your delayed awareness can be automatically but subjectively antedated or referred back in time, so you would report seeing the boy immediately (see Chapter 2, "Antedating of Delayed Sensory Experience").

Stepping on the brake is not a simple spinal reflex. It involves recognizing the nature of signal (in this case, a boy) and a decision to act, in order not to hit him. This fairly complex mental function is carried out unconsciously.

Perhaps we should clarify what we mean by unconscious (nonconscious) functions and how they differ from conscious mental functions. The prime feature of a conscious experience is awareness. This is a subjective phenomenon, accessible only to the individual with the experience. To study awareness, we must rely on the person's ability to indicate he has had such an experience. (A conscious experience also involves some content in the awareness—for example, being aware of or feeling a touch to the hand. The issue of content with and without awareness is considered elsewhere in the book (see Chapter 1, "Awareness," and the following section "Experimental Test of Time-On Theory"). We regard a psychological function or event as unconscious when the person has no reportable awareness for the event. This definition covers various possible kinds or levels of unconscious processes, from the depths of general anesthesia to so-called subconscious ones.

*Dreaming* is clearly a conscious process, even though the contents may contain distorted events. Dreams are usually poorly recalled or not recalled at all. Dreams are thus examples of awareness with little or no memory.

Many of the routine functional activities in the brain (and spinal cord) are carried out unconsciously. These include regulation of blood pressure and heart rate in relation to the level of exercise or emotional events; initiation and control of breathing; postural adjustments of the body and limbs; walking and running; control of gastrointestinal motility and secretions; regulation of endocrine glands (which secrete hormones); and even significant controls of the immune system. These kinds of maintenance functions occur at rest and in locomotion. They proceed while we eat, during sexual activities, during fight or flight responses, and so on. However, these kinds of activities are not properly referred to as mental or psychological. Indeed most of these activities do not and cannot ever reach into one's awareness.

Nevertheless, unconscious functions that do involve psychological or mental features are voluminous (see Velmans, 1991). *Conditioned reflexes* can be learned without the subject's awareness of the process. For example, the eyelid blinks reflexively in response to a puff of air to the eye. If a tone is sounded beginning a second or so before and ending during the puff of air, the subject learns to blink in response to the tone alone. The eminent psychologist Richard Thompson tells me he has conditioned the eyelid blink reflex *without any awareness* of the conditioning stimulus by the human subject. Other psychologists have also reported this phenomenon. Indeed, in a recent paper Clark and Squire (1998) report that if the conditioning tone ends 500 to 1,000 msec before the puff of air, the subjects can learn this conditioning *only if they are aware* of the stimuli. This 500-msec interval fits well with our evidence for the brain's requirement to produce awareness. Even the novelty of a change, in a complex learned sequence of stimuli, can be responded to without any awareness of that novelty by the human subject (Berns et al., 1997). Our quick reactions to sensory signals appear to be performed without any initial awareness of the signal.

Another experimental example is provided in studies of subjects reaching for a target that can shift its position. Each subject was asked to reach suddenly for a given target image or object. After the reaching movement began but before the target was touched, the location of the target was shifted. The subjects altered the direction of their reaching movements in "midstream" to touch the target at its new location. The interesting point here is that the subjects were not aware of making the midstream change in direction; the alteration was done unconsciously (Jeannerod, 1997).

Initiation of voluntary acts can arise unconsciously in the brain, well before any awareness of any conscious intention to move (see Chapter 4). That is, the brain starts the voluntary process unconsciously.

There is considerable evidence for many other simple and complex psychological (mental) activities that proceed unconsciously (for example, Kihlstrom, 1993, 1996; Shevrin and Dickman, 1980). Much of this evidence deals with findings that a person shows some mental effects of events even when there is no awareness of the events when they occurred. For example, words or drawings were displayed on a screen so briefly (say for 10 msec) that the subject had no awareness of those words or drawings. But when asked later to respond to *other* words or drawings, the subject's answers were clearly influenced by the earlier unconscious exposures.

There is also the commonly experienced phenomenon of having an intuitive feeling or hunch about an issue or decision. These hunches are based on unconscious, not conscious, mental backgrounds or perceptions. Haven't you had such intuitive hunches? In a recent direct study of the hunch phenomenon, Damasio et al. (1997) found that normal subjects could rather quickly learn to pick cards that "paid off" from the decks of cards that provided a successful payoff (two out of four decks). Subjects began to favor the money-making decks well before they could articulate any conscious strategy for their choice. Lowered skin resistance (presumably due to sweating or increased blood flow in the skin), a bodily indicator of anxiety, appeared during the time period in which the unconscious hunch was developing. This ability was found to be absent in six patients with damage to certain areas of the frontal lobes (of the cerebral cortex). General intelligence and memory were not impaired in these patients; instead, they were specifically deficient in the ability to make successful decisions, and to do that unconsciously! Nichols and Newsome (1999) have reviewed related evidence from experiments with monkeys. In these experiments, the animals quickly learned to choose the target that produced a higher reward, even though both targets were visually identical.

Even during general anesthesia for a surgical operation, there is evidence that conversation or suggestive comments can produce effects on "subsequent thoughts, feelings and actions without explicit recall of the events of surgery" (Bennett et al., 1985). These unconscious processes have been confirmed by a number of anesthesiologists. Of therapeutic importance is the observation that the nature of the surgeon's comments, received unconsciously by the anesthetized patient, can influence the course of later recovery. Positive statements can facilitate the later recovery while negative ones can disturb the recovery.

Many of our thought processes are apparently unconscious, particularly related to attempts to solve a problem. This is especially striking in dealing with a problem in mathematics, as described by some of the great mathematicians. For example, the famous mathematician Henri Poincaré (1913) was interested in how he arrived at mathematical solutions, and he kept notes about the process. He wrote that he was puzzled about how to solve a particularly difficult mathematical problem and, after some conscious mulling over the problem, he gave up on it. On a later trip to Lyon, the entire solution "popped" into his consciousness just as he stepped off the bus. Clearly, a great deal of unconscious yet creative thinking had gone on to produce that solution. It is also said that when mathematicians consciously perceive a solution to a difficult problem (this solution appearing after an unconscious process), they "know" intuitively whether that solution is correct, before consciously working out the necessary analytical proofs. The case for unconscious mental operations was also made by the renowned mathematician and philosopher, Alfred North Whitehead.

Creativity in general is almost certainly a function of unconscious or at least semiconscious mental processes. There are many anecdotal reports by great scientists of ideas for imaginative hypotheses of solutions to problems, which consciously appeared only after some period of *unconscious incubation*. Indeed, some of them describe an almost stereotyped sequence in producing new and original ideas of solutions: (1) specify the questions or problem; (2) gather or produce relevant information about the issue; (3) suspend further conscious attempts to produce an hypothesis that might lead to an answer (in other words, let the concern about the issue percolate at an unconscious level); (4) be attuned to the *conscious appearance* of a proper hypothesis of solution; and finally (5) apply a *conscious rational analysis* of what has finally arisen to a conscious level to test its usefulness and validity. Step (3) is probably the most creative one; the other steps are more in the nature of logical analysis. Poincaré argued that intuitive work is even more important than analytical work for the advancement of science. He said, "Pure logic does not lead to anything but tautologies; it creates nothing new" (as quoted by Rafael Franco, 1989).

Creative ideas have also been reported to appear in dreams and during daydreaming. Ideas and other thoughts that appear in dream states are clearly not the result of a deliberate conscious analysis or process. They appear with no immediate forethought and may be regarded as unconscious developments that pop into conscious awareness in the dream. There is the famous story of Otto Loewi, who was awarded a Nobel Prize for establishing that a chemical substance could be the transmitter at the (synaptic) junction between one nerve fiber and the next nerve or muscle cell. Loewi was frustrated by his inability to find a way to solve this question experimentally. Then one night he dreamt about a solution. He awoke and made some notes, and went back to sleep. The next morning he found he could not decipher his notes! When a similar dream appeared on a succeeding night, Loewi arose, went to his laboratory, and set up the imagined experiment immediately. The originality of the idea lay in collecting the fluid coming from one frog's heart and passing it into the intake of a second heart. When Loewi stimulated the vagus nerve to the first heart, producing a slowing or temporary stop of the first heart's beating, the second heart also exhibited a slowing of its rate. The second heart could only have received the "message" from the first heart by a chemical substance, released from its stimulated nerve and transported to the second heart. In subsequent years, such a chemical transmitter agency was found to apply to most other junctions between one nerve cell and the next, including those in the brain and spinal cord.

Creative writing, painting, musical composition, and performance are also widely believed to involve unconscious mental processes, but I shall not attempt to elaborate this view here. Arthur Koestler (1964) developed this view in *The Art of Creation*.

I have myself experienced numerous occasions in which productive new ideas have popped into my conscious mind when I was dreaming or daydreaming. For many years, I have been keeping a pad of paper and pencil at my bedside. When I wake up during the night with a novel idea, I make notes for possible daytime action. A number of interesting solutions and explanations for research problems have appeared from that source. I sometimes daydream when reading a book, taking a walk, listening to instrumental music, or even while listening to a lecture. For example, while I am listening to a live symphony performance, my mind often drifts off and other thoughts appear, perhaps stimulated in part by the background of good classical music. I scribble down any thoughts that appear to be creative solutions to an experimental or theoretical research problem, even in the darkness of the concert hall.

An example of a creative product of my daydreaming is the idea for using a reportable clock method to establish when a person becomes aware of voluntarily wanting to move (see Chapter 4). That occurred to me while I was sitting in my study room at the Rockefeller Center in Bellagio, Italy. I was supposed to be concentrating on writing a research paper on a quite different issue, one dealing with subjective antedating of a conscious sensory experience (Libet et al., 1979). The problem, of how experimentally to deal with the relation between brain processes and the conscious will to act, had reappeared the previous day during a discussion with my wife Fay about the apparent impossibility of solving that problem. The solution that popped into my mind was to instruct each subject to associate the first awareness of an intention to act with the position of the second hand of a clock. The subject's later report of that associated clock time could indicate the time at which the awareness appeared.

It is, in fact, important to allow your unconscious mental processes to develop ideas and solutions, and to provide opportunities for such processes to occur. Also, you must learn to recognize and pay attention to a product of these processes when it pops into conscious awareness. That is, you should allow for a free flow of unconscious processes and learn to trust in their importance. Such processes are often not stereotypic in nature; they are often creative. When you become aware of them, you can make conscious choices about how to use or deal with them. Alfred North Whitehead urged everyone to cultivate the habit of acting without thinking. He wrote, "Civilization advanced by extending the number of operations which we can perform without thinking about them" (quoted by Bruce Bower, 1999).

The importance of daydreaming for generating creative ideas and solutions is hard to get across convincingly to others. My wife often felt I was wasting my time and not "working" when she observed me sitting at my writing board and not writing much. I finally convinced her (I think) that such apparent inactivity was not a complete waste.

### Are Unconscious Functions "Mental"?

I have thus far avoided getting into a discussion of what is "mind" and what is a "mental" process. You can find very elaborate arguments on this topic in the literature, mostly by philosophers. As an experimental neuroscientist, I tend to take a simple direct approach that is in consonance with our reportable views and feelings about such concepts. According to dictionary definitions, "mind" refers to one's intellectuality but also to one's inclinations and impulses; in the latter sense, emotional processes are included.

"Mental" is simply the adjective for describing functions of "mind." Mind would thus subsume conscious experiences, but unconscious functions that fit into the definition would not be excluded. "Mind" might then be usefully regarded as an overall property of the brain that includes subjective conscious experiences and unconscious psychological functions.

But such a view has been strongly opposed by some. Philosopher John Searle (1993, p. 156) argues that "mental" should only apply to conscious subjective experience. He argues that unconscious functions are only accompanied by certain neuronal activities, without the necessity to invoke something else, namely an unconscious mental event. He agrees, however, that these activities could affect subsequent conscious thoughts, feelings, and behavior.

Well, then, why should we think of an unconscious psychologically significant process as a "mental" process? When we adopt that view, we are imparting an attribute to the unconscious process that makes it qualitatively akin in some ways to a conscious process, except that it lacks awareness. Both views (unconscious as mental or nonmental) are unproven hypotheses. But there are reasons for regarding the unconscious as a mental feature, as one that better describes the known attributes of unconscious functions. It also provides a more imaginative and potentially conjectural picture for dealing with these functions.

Unconscious functions deal with psychological issues in ways that seem basically similar to conscious functions except for the absence of awareness. Unconscious functions can be representations of experience (Kihlstrom, 1993). Cognitive, imaginative, and decision-making processes all can proceed unconsciously, often more creatively than in conscious functions. Unconscious psychologically significant functions of these kinds, like conscious ones, cannot be described or predicted by an *a priori* knowledge of the neuronal processes, contrary to Searle's view. It seems simpler, more productive, and more in tune with clinical experience to regard unconscious processes as "mental functions," phenomena that are related to the conscious mental functions but lack the added phenomenon of awareness. (After all, definitions are only useful insofar as they promote productive thinking about the item.) To add awareness to an unconscious function can occur when the duration of cortical activations is lengthened by up to 0.5 sec (see the following section).

### *Time-On Theory: How Does the Brain Distinguish between Conscious and Unconscious Mental Functions?*

Conscious and unconscious mental functions differ most importantly in the presence of awareness for the former and the absence of awareness in the latter. We found that the brain requires substantial time (about 0.5 sec) to "produce" awareness of a sensory signal, while unconscious functions appear to require much less time (100 msec or so). What was the brain doing during the shorter periods of activations that did not last long enough to produce awareness? Far from being silent, the brain exhibited recordable neuronal responses that resembled those that went on to finally become adequate for awareness. These shorter-lasting trains of nerve cell responses could not produce awareness. But, we asked, could they provide a mechanism for an unconscious detection of a sensory signal? That question led us to propose a time-on theory for explaining the transition between brain activities required for unconscious mental functions and those required for conscious functions.

The time-on theory has two simple components:

(1) To produce a conscious sensory experience (in other words, with awareness), appropriate brain activities must proceed for a minimum duration of about 500 msec (when the event is near threshold). That is, the time-on or duration of the activities is about 0.5 sec. We had already established this feature experimentally.

(2) We proposed that when these same brain activities have durations shorter than those required for awareness, they could

nevertheless be involved in producing an unconscious mental function, without awareness. An unconscious function might then be transformed into a conscious one simply by increasing the duration (time-on) of the appropriate brain activities. We realized that time-on was probably not the only factor in the transition between unconscious and conscious, but we saw it as a controlling factor.

You may ask, what is it that makes some time-ons long enough for awareness and most of the others not long enough? We don't have a full answer to that. However, there is good reason to believe that focusing attention on a given sensory signal may be an agent for making the sensory response a conscious one. We don't yet know what brain mechanism "decides" to focus attention on one signal and not on others. But there is evidence that the attention mechanism could "light up" or activate some areas of cerebral cortex; such an increase in excitability level of those areas might facilitate their lengthening the duration of their nerve cell responses to achieve the time-on for awareness.

We don't know precisely which neuronal activities are "appropriate," for either a conscious or unconscious mental event. But my argument is that whatever the appropriate nerve cell activities are, the duration of those activities may be a critical factor in determining the distinction between the two kinds of mental events.

*Experimental test of time-on theory.* Any theory proposed as scientific must be testable. So we designed and carried out an experimental test of the time-on theory (Libet et al., 1991). The test involved two features: (1) We had to be able to vary the duration of proper repetitive activations of the sensory cortex, so we could control the amount of time-on (duration) of nerve cell activities. That would allow us to deliver stimuli with *durations* below and above the 500 msec necessary to produce awareness; (2) We required a psychological task for the subject to indicate whether the input signal was or was not "perceived" (detected), regardless of awareness of the signal. That would allow us to match the duration of stimulus with both the accuracy of detection of the signal and the level of awareness that it did or did not produce in each trial. Any correct detection of the signal with no awareness of it would, of course, constitute an unconscious detection of the signal.

The first condition was met by applying stimulus trains to the ascending sensory pathway in the thalamus, below the sensory cortex. As shown earlier, with threshold liminal intensities, minimum durations of up to about 500 msec were required here also to elicit a conscious sensation. (We made the pulses somewhat stronger than the minimum threshold, so approximately 400-msec durations were needed instead of 500 msec). The actual *duration* of each train of 72 pulses per second was different for each testing trial, randomly ranging from 0 (no stimulus) to about 750 msec (that is, from 0 pulses to 55 pulses in this setting). A train duration of 500 msec would contain 36 pulses here.

The subject faced a panel containing two buttons, each of which could be lit up briefly (see Fig. 3.2). In each trial, light #1 ($L_1$) was lit for 1 sec; and 1 sec later, $L_2$ was lit for 1 sec. The stimulus to the sensory thalamus was applied in a random manner either during the time $L_1$ was lit or during the $L_2$ lighting.

The subject's task was to indicate in which of the two lit periods, $L_1$ or $L_2$, the stimulus was delivered. She had to make that decision even if she were not aware of any sensation produced

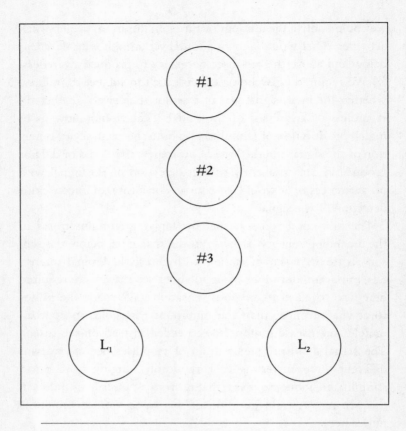

**Fig. 3.2.** Test of time-on theory. A box with this surface panel faced the subject. In each trial, light #1 ($L_1$) lit up for 1 sec; then light #2 ($L_2$) lit up for 1 sec. Stimulus was delivered during either $L_1$ or $L_2$ randomly in successive trials.

After the $L_2$ light was finished, the subject indicated whether the stimulus was delivered either during the $L_1$ or the $L_2$ light period by pressing the $L_1$ or $L_2$ button. Subject was instructed to do this even if he or she felt nothing in $L_1$ and $L_2$.

Subject then also indicated the level of *awareness* of the stimulus by pressing button #1, #2, or #3. Button #1: The subject felt the stimulus, even if weakly. Button #2: The subject had an "uncertain feeling of the stimulus; or, maybe something different," even if not the same sensation felt for #1. Button #3: The subject felt nothing and was guessing in choosing $L_1$ vs. $L_2$. From Libet et al., 1991. Reprinted with permission from Oxford University Press.

in the test. In other words, she was forced to make a choice. She indicated her choice by pressing the $L_1$ or $L_2$ button. She then pressed *other* buttons to report her level of awareness of the stimulus: Button #1 if she felt it, even weakly; #2 if she was not certain whether she felt it or if she felt anything different during the selected light; #3 if she felt nothing and was just guessing in choosing $L_1$ or $L_2$.

The choice of $L_1$ or $L_2$ should, by pure chance, produce correct responses in 50 percent of trials. Correct responses in more than 50 percent of trials, with a given stimulus duration, would indicate actual detection of the stimuli with that duration, whether with or without awareness of the signal. Each subject performed in hundreds of trials so the results could be statistically analyzed.

The results were very instructive: (1) For trials in which no stimulus (0 pulses) was delivered during either $L_1$ or $L_2$ the responses were indeed very close to 50 percent correct, as expected from chance alone. (2) For all trials in which a stimulus was delivered, but subjects were not aware of any sensation and were guessing, the correct responses were significantly greater than 50 percent. This was true even with short train durations of 15–150 msec (1 to 10 pulses). With longer stimulus trains (150 to 260 msec) and a guessing subject, subjects were 75 percent correct, and so on. Clearly, subjects were often detecting the stimulus and making a correct response *with no awareness* of any effect of the stimulus.

(3) By a statistical analysis, we determined the difference in stimulus durations between condition A (correct responses with guessing and *no* awareness) and condition B (correct responses with some minimal evidence of *awareness, at the uncertain level*). In both of these groups, A and B, all responses were correct.

The difference lay in the no awareness (guessing) in A, as opposed to minimal awareness of the stimulus in B. We found that to go from condition A (correct, but no awareness) to condition B (correct, with minimal awareness) required an additional stimulus duration of almost 400 msec. In other words, to add only awareness to a correct detection required an increase in stimulus duration of almost 400 msec for the repetitive train of pulses. This result was precisely as predicted by the time-on theory.

The results proved that awareness is a *phenomenon independent of content*. With content the same (correct report on presence of stimulus), an increase of 400 msec in stimulus duration was necessary to add minimal awareness to the response. This unique requirement for awareness *per se* makes it a function separate from others in the brain.

The results also provided direct evidence for a form of "subliminal perception." Shorter durations of cortical activations were subliminal in the sense that they did not produce awareness of the signal. Nevertheless, these subliminal inputs were responded to correctly at well above the 50 percent chance level. I consider the potential implications of this finding for subliminal perceptions generally in the following section (view 10). In any case, this result directly demonstrates the important distinction between *unconscious detection* of a signal and the *conscious awareness* of a signal.

The transition between unconscious detection and conscious awareness of the stimulus was here produced simply by a suitable increase in duration of identical cortical activations (via the direct ascending sensory pathway). The result gave us some confidence in the theory, and permits us to speculate on some important implications that follow from the time-on theory.

## How Time-On Theory Can Affect Our Mental Functions

Recall that in the time-on theory, the feature that adds awareness to an otherwise unconscious psychological function is a substantial increase in the duration (time-on) of the appropriate neuronal activities. The theory thus suggests or leads to the following views.

(1) Perhaps all conscious mental events actually *begin unconsciously* before any awareness appears. We already have the experimental evidence that this situation occurs in the case of awareness of a bodily sensation, and also for the internally generated awareness of the intention to perform a voluntary act (see Chapter 4). That is, to elicit any such awareness requires a substantial duration of cerebral activities. That means that unconscious, shorter-lasting cerebral activities have preceded the delayed conscious event. It seems likely that such a fundamental requirement, found by us for two different kinds of conscious experience, would also apply to other kinds of awareness—in other words, for the other sensory modalities (vision, hearing, smell, taste) and for conscious thoughts and feelings, emotional or otherwise.

Application of such a principle to internally generated thinking and emotional feelings introduces a very interesting attribute. Thoughts of various kinds, imaginations, attitudes, creative ideas, solving of problems, and so on initially develop unconsciously. Such unconscious thoughts only reach a person's conscious awareness if the appropriate brain activities last a long enough time.

(2) Vocalizing, speaking, and writing fall into the same category; that is, they are all likely to be initiated unconsciously. There is already experimental evidence that the cerebral electrical change (the readiness potential or RP) that begins unconsciously in a simple voluntary action also precedes these other voluntary actions of speaking or writing (see R. Jung, 1982). I discuss the impact of this finding for the nature of conscious will in Chapter 4. In the case of speech, for example, this means that the process to start speaking, and even the content of what is to be spoken, has been initiated and prepared unconsciously before the speaking begins. If the time-on requirement for awareness holds here, it would be manifestly impossible to rapidly speak a series of words, in the usual fashion, if one first had to become consciously aware of each word. When a spoken word is something different from what the speaker would *consciously* like to have said, he usually corrects that *after* hearing himself speak. Indeed, if you try to be aware of each word before speaking it, the flow of your speech becomes slow and hesitant.

In smoothly flowing speech, words are allowed to appear "on their own," in other words, they are initiated unconsciously. As E. M. Forster reportedly stated, "How can I tell what I think until I see what I say?" Then there is the event recounted by Bertrand Russell after a late night talk with Lady Ottoline. Russell wrote, "I did not know I loved you till I heard myself telling you so—for one instant I thought, 'Good God, what have I said?' and then I knew it was the truth." (These two examples were described in a paper by Sean Spence, 1996.) And, there is the elegant statement by writer E. L. Doctorow, "I love to have my mind flowing through sentences and making discoveries, to trust the gift of writing and see what it will deliver me in to." My daughter Gayla tells me that when she writes poetry, the first line or two just pop into her mind; thereafter, the rest of the poem flows out directly to her writing hand from an unconscious source.

(3) The playing of a musical instrument, like the piano or violin, or singing must also involve a similar *unconscious* performance of the actions. Pianists often play rapid musical runs in which the fingers of both hands are hitting the keys in sequences so fast that they can barely be followed visually. Not only that, each finger must hit the correct piano key in each sequence. It would be impossible for a pianist to become *consciously aware* of each finger's action if there were a substantial delay before awareness of each finger's movement. Indeed, performers report that they are not aware of the intention to activate each finger. Instead, they tend to focus their attention on expressing their musical feelings. Even these feelings arise *unconsciously,* before any awareness of them develops, based on our time-on principle for producing awareness. Instrumentalists and singers know that if they "think" about the music being performed, their expression becomes forced and stilted. Smoothly expressed music, with heartfelt and spiritual feelings, is produced when the performer allows the expression to arise without conscious specifications, in other words, to arise unconsciously. Musicians often close their eyes while performing; perhaps that action facilitates getting in touch with their unconscious feelings while reducing external signals. I have first-hand reports of all these factors from my four children, who are advanced string players, and from my own singing experience.

(4) All quick behavioral, motor responses to a sensory signal are performed unconsciously. These are responses that can be made within 100–200 msec after the signal, well before awareness of the signal could be expected. Many actions in sports fall

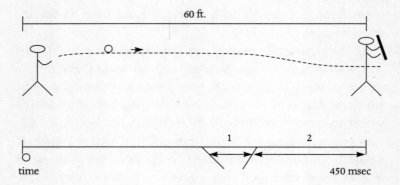

**Fig. 3.3.** Timings for baseball batter's response to a pitched ball. Say the pitcher delivers the ball at 90 mph with curved trajectory. The ball reaches the batter in 450 msec. The batter may wait until the final 200 msec (during the #1 period) to try to detect the course of the ball's movement to him.

The batter must decide whether to swing (#2 period) before the last 150 msec or so; the 150 msec is the minimum time required to activate the motor cortex, which sends a neural message down to the spinal motor-nerve cells that activates the appropriate muscles in about 50 msec; the actual muscle contractions that produce the swing of the bat occur in about 100 msec. The great homerun hitters, like the current champion Barry Bonds, can swing the bat with extraordinary speed. That enables them to delay their decision to swing until the minimum required time to hit the ball.

into this category. A professional tennis player must respond to a ball served to him at 100 mph and with a curving trajectory. These players report being aware of the serving motion pattern of the opponent, but they are not immediately aware of the ball's location when hitting the return. A baseball batter faces a pitched ball at 90 mph (132 ft/sec), with the ball curving or sinking at the last moment. He must decide whether to hit that ball and to swing the bat in a path that can meet the ball (see Fig. 3.3). Because the pitcher is 60 ft from the batter, the ball reaches the batter in a total of 450 msec. The batter has only the last 200 or so msec of the ball's approach to recognize the speed and trajectory of the ball and to make the decision to swing. Both that recognition and decision are presumably initially unconscious. Great baseball hitters are probably those who can successfully delay these processes as much as is physiologically possible. Once the baseball batter has made his decision and begun to swing, it is remarkable that he usually cannot stop his swing if he realizes it was the wrong choice.

I might even add that great athletes, in general, are those who can let their unconscious mind take over without interference from the conscious mind. Athletes tell us that if they try "to think" (become aware) of immediate responses, they become less successful. Indeed, I am tempted to generalize that this is true for all creative processes, in art, science, and mathematics.

Quick responses to signals can be measured quantitatively in reaction times (RT) studies. In an RT study, the actual responses are presumably made unconsciously, with awareness of the signal following the act. It has, in fact, been shown that reaction time to a given signal can be the same even when awareness of the signal is completely obliterated. This obliteration can be produced by applying a delayed masking stimulus following the initial signal for which reaction time is measured (Taylor and McCloskey, 1990).

(5) Unconscious mental functions can proceed at higher speed, if they are carried out by shorter-lasting neuronal activities. Judging from our experiments on signal detections and forced choice responses with no awareness of the signal, the effective time-on for neural activities in unconscious functions can be very short indeed—about 100 msec or less. This implies that the series of unconscious processes involved in solving a problem can proceed speedily, each brief process after another. Such

rapidity obviously helps make unconscious thought very effective. It consists of short-lasting elements of unconscious thought sweeping along to accomplish a series of difficult steps in a complex problem. By contrast, if a person did not proceed until awareness appeared for each step in a series of thoughts, the whole process would be slowed down by a factor of five or so, and conscious thoughts and resulting decisions to act would become a plodding affair.

(6) The appearance of a conscious experience has an all-or-nothing character (see Fig. 2.2). That is, there is no reportable conscious awareness of an event even if the appropriate neuronal activities persist for as much as 90 percent of the 500 msec required for actual threshold awareness. What the time-on experiments have demonstrated is that threshold awareness pops in rather suddenly when the activities persist for the full 500-msec requirement!

(7) The popular notion that people have a continuous stream of consciousness is contradicted by the time-on requirement for conscious awareness. The notion of a stream of consciousness was proposed by the great psychologist William James, on the basis of his intuitive grasp of his own conscious thoughts. Many psychologists and writers of fiction have adopted the view of a stream of consciousness as an authentic characteristic of a subject's or character's mental activities. But our evidence indicates that *conscious thought processes* must *consist of discontinuous separate events*. If the beginning of each conscious event only appears after a substantial delay, incurred by a required 500-msec period of neuronal activations, then a series of conscious events would not appear in a continuous stream. Awareness in each conscious event is not present in the initial 500 msec or so.

Discontinuity in a series of conscious events is a counterintuitive feature. It is not what people experience; we do not perceive a choppiness in our conscious life. In the case of sensory experiences, our feeling of continuity may be explained by the automatic subjective referral of each experience back in time to the fast-evoked response of the sensory cortex, a response that occurs within 10–20 msec of the sensory stimulus. Subjectively, we do not perceive any appreciable delay in our awareness of sensory events. Our experiment showed that people thought they were aware of a sensory stimulus about 500 msec before they could possibly have become aware of the stimulus. This discrepancy became known to us objectively; it is no longer a theoretical speculation. We called this phenomenon "subjective referral of conscious sensory awareness backward in time" (see Chapter 2).

However, this feature cannot be applied to all other kinds of conscious experiences, including the conscious intention to act and thought events generally. We (Libet et al., 1979) proposed subjective antedating (referral backward in time) only for sensory experiences. Even in that case, antedating occurs only when the sensory input elicits a fast timing signal in the sensory cortex, the primary evoked potential (see Chapter 2). In the case of the endogenous appearance of a conscious voluntary intention to act, we have experimentally demonstrated that the subjective timing of that experience is in fact delayed by about 400 msec or more after the onset of the brain activity that leads to the voluntary act (Chapter 4). Conscious intention to act, with no external cues to instigate it, is an example of a conscious experience that arises within the brain (in other words, endogenously). There is no primary evoked potential here, as there is in the sensory system's responses to stimuli that are not endogenous in origin.

Perhaps our subjective feeling of a smooth flow in a series of

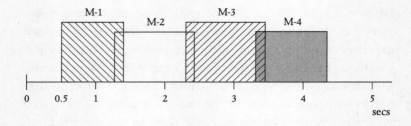

**Fig. 3.4.** Overlap of discontinuous mental events and the feeling of a smooth stream of consciousness.

M-1 conscious mental event begins suddenly after a 500-msec period of unconscious initiating processes. M-2 conscious mental event may *begin* after its unconscious initiating processes but before the end of M-1. Similarly for M-3 and M-4.

The overlapping of the successive conscious mental events avoids breaks in the stream of consciousness.

thoughts is explainable by an *overlapping* of the different mental events (see Fig. 3.4). The brain appears capable of several conscious events occurring almost simultaneously, overlapping in time. To illustrate how discontinuities of underlying events can still produce a smoothly continuous overall product, think about the physiology of muscle action. A skeletal muscle, like the biceps in the arm, is made up of many motor units, each containing many individual muscle cells or fibers. When you perform a smooth contraction of the biceps, like bending or flexing the elbow, an electrical recording of any single motor unit's actions would show that it is "popping off" at a relatively low rate of roughly ten times a second. Direct studies of individual motor responses show that the muscle contractions at ten times per second are jumpy or wave-like, not smoothly sustained contractions. The smoothly sustained overall contraction of the whole biceps muscle is therefore explained as the result of an *asyn-*

*chrony* in the activations of the nerve fibers that activate different motor units in the biceps. The wave-like contractions of different individual motor units then overlap in time, so the relaxation phase in one unit is accompanied by a contraction phase in another, and so on. If we electrically stimulate the whole motor nerve to the biceps at a rate of ten per second, we can force all the motor units to respond synchronously at this rate. The synchronized contractions at ten per second in fact do produce a jumpy, tremor type of contraction of the whole biceps muscle.

(8) The time-on requirement for conscious experiences may serve a "filter function" to limit conscious experiences at any one time. It is clear that very few out of the thousands of sensory inputs delivered per second to the brain achieve conscious awareness, though they may lead unconsciously to meaningful cerebral and psychological responses. The French philosopher Henri Bergson proposed that the brain may block most sensory inputs from access to consciousness to protect us from being overwhelmed by conscious responses to them. Our present experimental findings may provide a physiological mechanism to achieve that blocking.

We propose, then, that the large majority of sensory inputs remain unconscious because they do not develop a sufficiently long duration (time-on) of the appropriate cerebral nerve cell activities. Perhaps it is the attention mechanism that allows a given selected response to last long enough to elicit awareness; but attention itself is apparently not a sufficient mechanism for awareness. Thus, the time-on requirement for awareness could provide part of the mechanism for screening out sensory inputs, which do not reach awareness.

The screening or filtering of inputs prevents conscious awareness from becoming cluttered and permits it to be focused on just a few events or issues at a time. If you were to become aware of all sensory inputs, you would be overloaded with an ineffective buzz of conscious events. Perhaps some mental disorders reflect improper functioning of such a filter mechanism, by an abnormal reduction in the duration of brain activities required for awareness.

(9) Unconscious detection of a signal should be clearly distinguished from conscious awareness of the signal. This distinction was directly demonstrated by the results of the experiment previously described as a test of the time-on theory. But the distinction is often overlooked, leading to confusing and erroneous conclusions about the nature of conscious experience. Studies based on signal detection theory find that subjects respond correctly, in other words, at better than chance levels, to stimulus signals with intensities down near zero. This has led to the conclusion that there is virtually no threshold level required to elicit a (conscious) sensory perception; accuracy of responses increases smoothly along a curve relating accuracy to stimulus intensity, the latter starting from zero. That conclusion precisely matches our results for *unconscious detection* of sensory inputs, without awareness. In studies of signal detection (Green and Swets, 1966) and of many other psychophysical issues, subjects are asked to make a forced-choice response. In a forced choice, the subject is asked to answer "yes" or "no" to a question about the stimulus; she is not asked about whether she was aware of the stimulus. The two different questions can produce strikingly different results.

The forced-choice question, strictly speaking, studies *detection* of a signal, whether unconscious or accompanied by awareness. A couple of interesting examples illustrate this: Vallbö et al. (1984) found that, for sensory input from the skin, the absolute minimum possible message could probably be perceived. That minimum is a single nerve impulse in a single sensory nerve fiber. But the forced-choice response by the subject was a "yes" or "no" as to whether some sensory message was delivered. Vallbö himself has agreed that this did not reflect sensory awareness, and that it was probably a case of *unconscious sensory detection* (personal communication). But many neuroscientists have been erroneously regarding his finding as an indicator of an absolute potentiality for *conscious* sensory perception.

Human subjects can discriminate between two vibratory stimuli of different frequencies to the skin. This can occur even when the time intervals, between the individual repetitive vibratory pulses, are much less than the 500-msec time period we have found necessary for threshold awareness of a sensory event. It has therefore been argued, by some, that our evidence for the long time to awareness cannot be correct, because we can tell the difference between vibrations that each have much shorter intervals between pulses. But the ability to discriminate between short time intervals between vibratory pulses at different frequencies demonstrates a detection of these differences; awareness of that discrimination comes later, in our view. That is, my question is, *when* is the subject aware of the discrimination, not how short an interval between pulses can he detect?

The reports of blindsight by Lawrence Weiskrantz (1986) provide a beautiful example of the distinction between unconscious detection and conscious awareness. Patients were studied who had lost their conscious vision in some part of their visual field, due to damage of the visual cortex. When asked to point to a target in that blind area, even if they were guessing, they did so with remarkable accuracy but reported they could not see the target.

(10) Subliminal perception: If a subliminal stimulus is defined as one of which the person is not consciously aware, there is clearly a potentiality for unconscious detection of that subliminal stimulus. Direct evidence for this appeared in our experimental test of the time-on theory (see discussion earlier in this chapter). Subliminal perception is less easily proven when ordinary natural sensory stimuli are used. This is because the differences (of strength, duration, and so on) between a subliminal and a supraliminal (awareness-producing) sensory stimulus are usually small. However, a considerable amount of indirect evidence supports the existence of subliminal perceptions. These mostly deal with the alterations in later tests, applied after an exposure to stimuli whose content did not reach conscious awareness. The subject's responses to the later tests show an influence of the previous subliminal stimuli that themselves produced no awareness. In an early study, Howard Shevrin (1973) flashed visual drawings or words so briefly (1–2 msec) that the subjects were completely unaware of the content in that flash. Yet later tests showed that these subliminal contents had an effect on the subject's choices of responses in tests of word associations; the subjects remained unaware of these effects. Many other analogous tests have been reported in which subliminal word stimuli "primed" the later responses of the subjects in test situations.

(11) Where in the brain do unconscious and conscious functions take place? Are there different locations for these two aspects of mental function? The time-on theory suggests that unconscious and conscious functions could both be mediated in the *same brain areas,* by the same group of neurons. If the transition between the two functions is simply one of a longer duration of similar nerve cell activities to elicit awareness, we need not postulate separate neuron entities for each. It is, of course,

possible that more than one stage or area of brain activity partic-ipates in mediating conscious mental processes and that some of these areas are different for unconscious functions. In such a case, the single area with time-on control may not represent the only distinction between unconscious and conscious function. However, the time-on feature could still be a controlling factor for the distinction, in whatever areas of the brain it is operative.

The phenomenon of blindsight(see Weiscrantz, 1986), raises the possibility of separate pathways and brain structures for con-scious and unconscious functions. A human patient with a lesion in the primary arousal area of the cerebral cortex is blind; that is, he has no conscious vision for the external visual field that is normally represented in the area that is destroyed. Nevertheless, such patients can correctly point to an object in that visual field when asked to do that simply as a forced choice. The subjects re-port that they do not consciously see that object.

The unconscious blindsight action may be carried out by an area or network in the brain that is different from that for con-scious vision (for which the primary visual area is necessary). However, in an alternative explanation, both the conscious and unconscious visual functions may "reside" in some structure outside the primary visual cortex, for example, in some second-ary visual area. The function of the primary visual cortex might then be to fire inputs repetitively to this secondary area, thereby increasing the duration of the activities there so as to add aware-ness to the visual response. This effect would be absent when the primary visual area is not functional.

Can you have conscious perception without the primary vi-sual area (V1)? In a very interesting study, Barbur et al. (1993) claimed to have shown that one can. They studied a patient who had lost area V1 completely, by damage in a car accident. He exhibited classical blindness in the visual hemi-field corresponding to the destroyed V1 area. Nevertheless, he was able to discriminate the direction of motion of visual stimuli. He also "showed, through his verbal reports, that he is consciously aware of both the nature of the visual stimulus and its direction of motion."

However, Barbur et al.'s conclusion—that conscious visual perception is possible in the absence of V1—does not exclude our time-on theory. It is possible that area V5, which shows increased activity in response to the visual stimuli, may achieve production of visual *awareness* by virtue of a sufficiently long duration of activations. Indeed, Barbur et al. (1993) delivered visual stimuli repetitively during substantial periods of time.

(12) Modulation of the content of a conscious experience is recognized as an important process in psychology and psychiatry. It is most directly demonstrable when a person reports an experience that *differs* from the actual visual image presented. Persons who are emotionally disturbed by the sight of a nude woman may report seeing an altered version of the nude picture shown to them. (An eminent Swedish neurologist was asked if he had tried this particular example on his subjects. He replied that nude pictures would not be adequate as psychological troublemakers in Sweden.) The alteration in content of the experience appears not to be one of conscious distortion; the subject is unaware of his distortion of the image and the process appears to be an unconscious one.

Freud, of course, made use of the modulatory phenomenon in his views of the unconscious effects of emotional conflicts on a person's conscious experience and verbal expressions (see Shevrin, 1973). The time-on theory provides a physiological opportunity in which unconscious modulations of the content of an experience can occur. To effect a change in the subjective content of a presented image, some time after the stimulus is required. If you were to become conscious of a sensory image immediately, there would be no opportunity for unconscious alteration of the conscious image. During the time interval, before conscious sensory awareness appears, brain patterns could detect the image and react to it, by producing activities that modify the content of the conscious experience before it appears.

Our evidence indicates that a substantial period of neural activity (500 msec of time-on) is in fact required to elicit awareness of the sensory event. That delay provides a simple and sufficient physiological opportunity during which unconscious brain patterns can alter the content of the experience before awareness of it appears! Indeed, the experimental phenomenon of subjective referral of a conscious sensory experience backward in time provides relatively direct evidence for one kind of modulatory distortion of the subjective experience. The delayed experience is subjectively timed as if it were not delayed at all. Our further experimental findings showed that the subjective experience of a skin stimulus could be reported to be distinctly *stronger* than it actually was, when that skin stimulus was followed by a *delayed cortical stimulus* that started as much as 500 msec later (see Chapter 2). That is direct evidence that the time period (500 msec) in which the sensory experience is being finally brought into awareness can be used to alter the content of the experience before it reaches awareness.

Any modulations or modifications of the developing experience would be unique to the person involved. It would reflect the person's own history of experiences and his emotional and moral make up. But the modulations are made unconsciously! Consequently, one may say that the unique nature of a given person can express itself in unconscious processes. This is in accord with the proposals of Sigmund Freud and with much of clinical psychiatry and psychology.

We can see, then, how the discovery of a relatively simple neuronal time requirement for producing awareness (the time-on factor) can have penetrating impacts on our view of the ways in which a variety of unconscious and conscious mental functions operate. It is important to note that these neuronal time factors could only have been discovered by direct experiments on how the brain deals with conscious experience, not by speculative theories based on previous knowledge of brain processes.

# 4

## INTENTION TO ACT: DO WE HAVE FREE WILL?

How the brain deals with voluntary acts is an issue of fundamental importance to the role of conscious will and, beyond
that, to the question of free will. It has been commonly assumed
that in a voluntary act, the conscious will to act would appear
before or at the start of the brain activities that lead to the act. If
that were true, the voluntary act would be initiated and specified
by the conscious mind. But, what if that were not the case? Is it
possible that the specific brain activities leading to a voluntary
act begin *before* the conscious will to act, in other words, before
the person is *aware* that he intends to act? This possibility has
arisen partly from our evidence that sensory awareness is delayed by a substantial time period of brain activities. If the internally generated awareness of the will or intention to act also is
delayed by a required period of activities lasting up to about 500
msec, it seems possible that the brain's activities that initiate a
willed act begin well before the conscious will to act has been
adequately developed.

We were able to examine this issue experimentally. What we
found, in short, was that the brain exhibited an initiating process, beginning 550 msec before the freely voluntary act; but

awareness of the conscious will to perform the act appeared only 150–200 msec before the act. The voluntary process is therefore initiated unconsciously, some 400 msec before the subject becomes aware of her will or intention to perform the act. The experimental evidence for this surprising sequence is given in this chapter.

## Experimental Design

The possibility of an experimental investigation of this question was opened by a discovery made by Kornhuber and Deecke (1965). They found that a recordable electrical change in brain activity regularly and specifically preceded a voluntary act. A voluntary act was preceded by a slow rise in electrical negativity, recordable at an area of the scalp located predominantly at the vertex, the top of the head. The electrical change started about 800 msec or more *before* a subject performed an apparently voluntary act. It was therefore called the *readiness potential* (RP) or, in German, the Bereitschaftspotential.

The act under study was a sudden bending or flexion of the wrist or fingers. Each RP is very small and virtually buried among the other electrical activities of the resting brain. Therefore, many such acts had to be performed to produce a computer-averaged tracing that summated the small RPs. The subject was allowed to perform these numerous acts in a "self-paced" manner. But his own choosing of times to act was limited by the period of about 6 sec that was allowed by Kornhuber and Deecke for each trial, in order to achieve the summation of 200–300 RPs within an acceptable experimental time period.

Kornhuber and Deecke did not consider the question of when the conscious will to act appeared, in relation to the brain's preparation (the RP). But the long time by which the RP precedes the voluntary act suggested to me, intuitively, that there might be a discrepancy between the *onset of brain* activity and the time of appearance of the *conscious* intention to perform the voluntary act. In a public discussion of willed actions, the neuroscientist and Nobel laureate Sir John Eccles stated his belief that an RP starting >800 msec before a voluntary act must mean that the associated conscious intention appears even before that early beginning of the RP. I realized that there was no evidence to support Eccles's view, which was presumably colored by his own philosophy of mind-brain interaction (see Popper and Eccles, 1977).

Establishing the time of the conscious will relative to the onset of brain activity (the RP) was clearly important. If conscious will were to follow the onset of RP, that would have a fundamental impact on how we view free will. But, at the time, I saw no way to test the issue experimentally. It seemed impossible to achieve a valid measurement of the time of appearance of conscious intention. Conscious will is a subjective phenomenon, not directly accessible to external observations. It requires a report by the human subject who is experiencing that subjective event. Having the subject press a button or say "now" to indicate his conscious intention would add further voluntary acts to the wrist flexion being studied. That would obscure the valid timing of the conscious will for the test act, relative to the brain activity. Also, there was no assurance that pressing a button or saying "now" as quickly as possible would be performed consciously. That is, the subject might make this quick response unconsciously, before becoming *aware* of the experience. If so, we would not have a valid time for the conscious will.

While I was a Resident Scholar at the Rockefeller Center for

Advanced Studies in Bellagio, Italy, in 1977, my thoughts returned to this apparently intractable problem in measurement. It then occurred to me that a subject could report the "clock-time" for her experience of the conscious intention to act. The clock time would be noted silently and reported after each trial was over. Upon returning to San Francisco, we devised such a technique (Libet et al., 1983).

A cathode ray oscilloscope was arranged to have its spot of light revolve near the outer edge of its face. The outer edge of the oscilloscope tube face was marked in clock seconds, sixty as usual, around the circle. The movement of the light spot was designed to simulate the sweep of the second hand of a usual clock. But our light spot completed the circle in 2.56 sec, about twenty-five times faster than the normal 60 sec (see Fig. 4.1). Each marked clock second therefore corresponded to about 43 msec of the spot's motion. This faster "clock" could then reveal time differences in hundreds of milliseconds.

The subject was seated about 2.3 m from the oscilloscope. For each trial, the subject fixed his gaze on the center of the oscilloscope's face. He was asked to perform a freely voluntary act, a simple but sudden flexion of the wrist at any time he felt like doing so. He was asked not to preplan when to act; rather he should let the act appear "on its own." That would allow us to separate the process for planning an act from that for a freely spontaneous will to "act now." He was also asked to associate his *first awareness* of his intention or wish to move with the "clock position" of the revolving light spot. That associated clock time was reported by the subject *after* completion of the trial. We labeled these reported times "W," for consciously wanting or wishing or willing to act. The RP produced in each such voluntary act was also recorded, with suitable electrodes on the

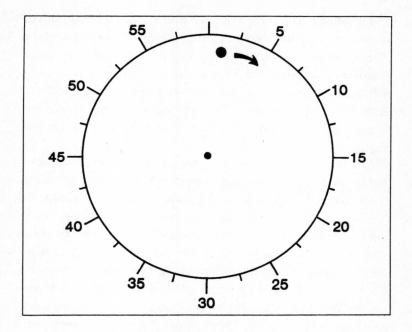

**Fig. 4.1.** The "clock" for timing a mental event. A spot of light, generated in a cathode ray oscilloscope, is arranged to move around the edge of the face of the oscilloscope, completing the circle in 2.56 sec. That simulates the sweep second hand of the usual clock, but moves about twenty-five times faster.

Numbers around the periphery represent seconds for the usual 60-sec sweep, but each marked second actually corresponds to about 43 msec here. Described in Libet et al., 1983.

head. An RP averaged over forty trials was found suitable. The time of onset of this averaged RP could then be compared to the reported W times averaged for the same forty acts.

We had serious doubts initially that the subjects could report their clock times of conscious intention with sufficient accuracy and reliability. As it turned out, we gained evidence that both of these characteristics were in a range adequate for our purposes. The W times reported for each group of forty trials exhibited a standard error (S.E.) of close to 20 msec. That was true for every subject, even though the averaged Ws differed among subjects. Because averaged Ws for all subjects was about −200 msec (before the motor act), an S.E. of ±20 msec provided adequate reliability.

A test for accuracy of W was a bit trickier to devise. We could not know, in an absolute way, how close the reported W was to the actual subjective time of that awareness. But we could test how accurately the subjects were using our clock time technique. For this, a series of forty trials was run in which a weak skin stimulus was delivered to the hand. The subjects were asked *not* to perform any voluntary act but rather to note the clock time of the skin sensation, to be reported after each trial (as for W). The skin stimulus was delivered at random clock times for the forty trials. These times ("S") were, of course, unknown to the subject, but they did become known to us observers in the computer printouts. We could thus compare an objectively known expected time of a subjective awareness with the clock times reported by the subject. The reported S times were close to the actual stimulus times. But they did show a difference of about −50 msec (in other words, earlier) from the actual delivered stimulus times. Because this difference was fairly consistent, it could be subtracted as a bias element from the average W of −200 msec. That produced a "corrected" average W of −150 msec. A series testing reported times of a skin stimulus was run in each session.

Our definition of a voluntary act included the following: The will to act arose endogenously. That is, there were no external cues for performing the act; no external limitations on when to perform the act; and most importantly, the subject felt she was responsible for the act and also felt that she could control when to act as well as whether or not to act. Human subjects can distinguish this last criterion from situations in which a motor act is produced without such a qualification. The neurosurgeon Wilder Penfield (see Penfield and Rasmussen, 1950) electrically stimulated the exposed motor cortex during surgery to treat epileptic foci. Stimulating the motor cortex produces contractions of some muscles and some movements in specific sites in the body. The patients reported that they did not will such movements; they reported that these actions were imposed on them by the stimulator, they were not voluntary.

There are numerous clinical disorders in which actions occur in the absence of conscious will. These include the involuntary actions in cerebral palsy, Parkinsonism, Huntington's chorea, Tourette's syndrome, and even obsessive compulsions to act. A striking example is the "alien hand sign" (Goldberg and Bloom, 1990). Patients with a lesion in a fronto-medial portion of premotor area of cerebral cortex may find that the hand and arm on the affected side perform curious purposeful actions, such as undoing a buttoned shirt when the subject is trying to button it up. All of this occurs without, or even against, the subject's intention and will.

### Two Groups of RP Onset Times

Our experimental objective was to study freely voluntary acts, performed with no external restrictions as to *when* to act. In most of our series, each of forty trials, there were no reports of preplanning by the subjects. These voluntary acts were completely free and performed spontaneously, without any preplanning of when to act. The nature of the act, sudden flexion of the wrist, was of course prescribed by us for the subject. That allowed us to place recording electrodes on the actual muscle to be activated; the recorded electromyogram gave us the time of the act and also served as a trigger to the computer to record the scalp potential that had appeared during the 2 to 3 sec prior to the muscle activation. But the time of the act was completely free for the subjects' own will. Our experimental question was: Does the conscious will to act precede or follow the brain's action? Testing this required only that the *timing* of the act be left freely up to the subject. The nature of the act was not important for that question.

For some series of trials the subjects reported having *preplanned* a range of clock time in which they would act, in spite of our encouragement not to do that. Those series produced RPs (#I) with earlier onsets, averaging about −800 to −1,000 msec (before the motor act) (Fig. 4.2). These values were similar to those reported by Kornhuber and Deecke and by others for their "self-paced" movements. For this and other reasons, it appeared that "self-paced" acts, done with certain limitations imposed by the experimenter, probably involved some preplanning by the subject of when to act. Their subjects knew they should perform the act within 6 sec, and that may have encouraged some preplanning of when to act. Our subjects had no such restriction.

In those series of forty acts in which the subject reported *no* preplanning of when to act, the onset of RPs (#II) averaged −550 msec (before activation of the muscle). It should be noted that the actual initiating process in the brain probably starts before our recorded readiness potential, RP, in an unknown

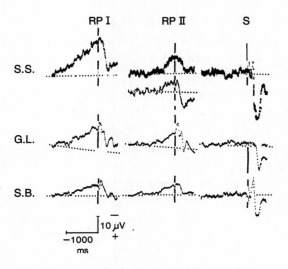

**Fig 4.2.** Readiness potentials (RP) preceding self-initiated voluntary acts. Each horizontal row gives the computer-averaged electrical potential recorded with an active electrode on the scalp, either at the midline vertex, for subjects G. L. and S. B., or on the left side (contralateral to the performing right hand) over the motor/premotor area that controls the hand, for subject S. S.

RPs labeled type II were found when every act (quick flexion of the wrist) in the series of forty trials was subjectively reported to originate spontaneously, with no preplanning of when to act. Type I RPs were those recorded when the subjects experienced a preplanning to act some time within the next second or so.

In column S, a near-threshold skin stimulus was applied in each of forty trials, at randomized times unknown to the subject. The subject was asked to recall and report, after each trial, the clock time when he became aware of the skin stimulus. This was similar to the reporting for awareness of the time of wanting to move. The large positive ERP (event-related-potential), with a peak at about 300 msec after the stimulus, is commonly observed when there is uncertainty about the stimulus (timing, in this case).

The solid vertical line in each tracing represents "O" time, at which the activation of the muscle has begun (indicated by an electromyogram, EMG) in RP series, or the time at which the skin stimulus was delivered in the S series. From Libet et al., 1982. Reprinted with permission from Elsevier, *Electroencephalography and Clinical Neurophysiology*, vol. 54, pp. 322–335.

area that then activates the supplementary motor area in the cerebral cortex. The supplementary motor area is located in the midline near the vertex and is thought to be the source of our recorded RP.

W values, for times of first awareness of the wish to act, averaged −200 msec for *all* series. (This could be corrected to −150 msec by the reporting error of −50 msec found for the S (skin stimulus) series.) W times were the same whether they were associated with RPI or RPII. That is, W times were the same whether there was or was not any preplanning of when to act! That indicated that the final volitional process (to "act now") starts at about −550 msec; it is the same, whether fully spontaneous or preceded by deliberations or preplanning of when to act. This final process may be the "act now" feature in a voluntary process, and the events in the "act now" feature are similar, regardless of preplanning.

The "act now" process should be distinguished from deliberations and advance making of choices about performing an act. One can, after all, deliberate all day and never act. We did not study the deliberation phase of volition, except for the occasional preplanning by our subjects of when to act.

There have been questions about the meaning of our W times. Because we produced evidence for a delay (up to 500 msec) for the development of a conscious sensory experience, awareness of the clock time may have started well before the conscious W report. But our subjects were asked to note the clock time associated with their first awareness of the wish to act; they were not asked to report the time when they became conscious of that association. There was presumably a delay of up to 500 msec before the conscious time appeared; but the automatic backward referral or antedating to the initial sensory signal of the associated clock time would allow the subject to feel he was aware at the time of association. In any case, we have no difficulty reading a clock time fairly correctly, as seen in our tests of reported times for a skin stimulus.

Robert Doty (personal communication) raised a different potential source of error in the interpretation of our W values. This involved the "cost" in extra time for switching attention to another task. The extra time required for switching tasks can be up to 100 msec or much longer in some instances. As applied to our case, "one cannot simultaneously attend to the introspective world of decision (to act) and to the position of the dot (clock-time) on the CRO (cathode ray oscilloscope)." Doty then suggested that the subject's free will starts the RP; when attention is turned to the oscilloscope clock, there is the cost in switching to this task. That could result in a belated report of W for an event that actually was observed at the start of the RP.

My reply to the switching task argument is as follows: (1) W delay from the onset of RPII was, as corrected, 400 msec. That is longer than the usual cost of switching tasks, even if such a cost exists here. (2) The conditions in our trials were quite different from those in the reports of costs for switching tasks. In the latter reports, the switch in tasks took place in completely separate trials. In our case, the subject was already fully instructed before the trial. Our task, given in advance, was to watch for the earliest experience of the urge or wish to act (W) while observing the "clock" continuously so as to associate the occurrence of W with the clock position. This all happened in the same trial, with task requirements that were different from those reported as producing a cost for switching. (3) RPI (when there is some preplanning of when to act) had an onset of about −800 to −1,000 msec; RPII (with spontaneous unplanned acts) had an onset of

—550 msec. Yet the W values in both cases were the same, at about −200 msec uncorrected. That means that Ws follow onsets of RPI by 600 to 800 msec; but Ws follow RPII by 350 msec. Both kinds of trials involve similar tasks, and similar costs of switchings in tasks if that applies here. But then, you cannot account for the difference in RP-W intervals, in the manner suggested by Doty. That is, you can't have W actually starting the RP, and appearing much later after onset of RPI than after RPII, if any costs in switching are the same for both cases. (4) Finally, the trials with skin stimuli (instead of movements) appear to eliminate the switching cost suggestion. The tasks in the stimulus series were essentially the same as those in voluntary act series. Subjects were asked to monitor the "clock" spot and to associate the position of the clock spot when they felt the weak skin sensation produced by the stimulus at randomly different times in different trials. The subjects in fact reported clock times that were very close to the actual times of the stimulus delivery; the reports averaged −50 msec, relative to actual stimulus time. This degree of accuracy does not allow for costs of switching in the hundreds of milliseconds.

## Sequence of Events in the "Act Now" Situation

So, what answer did we obtain to our original question, about relative timings for onset of brain activity (RP) versus conscious will to act? The clear answer was: The brain initiates the voluntary process *first*. The subject later becomes consciously *aware* of the urge or wish (W) to act, some 350 to 400 msec *after* the onset of the recorded RP produced by the brain. This was true for every series of forty trials with every one of the nine subjects.

This sequence of events has been confirmed by Keller and Heckhausen (1990), Haggard and Eimer (1999), and by two other groups, even though these two did not replicate our experiment precisely. Haggard and Eimer added interesting experimental features: They not only recorded the RP at the vertex (as we did), but also the RPs exhibited by the lateral premotor areas of cortex. These lateral RPs (LRP) had onsets closer to the $-550$ msec seen in our RPII recordings. Haggard and Eimer also divided the LRP trials into a group with the earlier onsets and one with the later onsets. The reported W values (time of awareness of the urge to act) for the earlier LRPs were also the earlier W values, and the Ws for later LRPs were in a later group of timings. However, in *both* groups of trials, the onsets of LRPs preceded the W times in the respective group. That showed the finding of LRP onsets preceding the W timings by substantial values is valid throughout the range of values for both the LRPs and Ws.

Haggard and Eimer made an additional point: They contend that the vertex RP process cannot have a causal relation to the appearance of W, because their RPs did not covary with their early versus late Ws. But our RPII is the significant value to be related to final initiation of the voluntary "act now" process. (RPI starts with a deliberation of when to move; that is a separate process.) Therefore, it is our RPIIs that should be divided into early and late groups, to test for covariance with early and late Ws. This measurement has not been made, either by us or by Haggard and Eimer, and so no conclusion about causation on these grounds can be presently drawn (see Haggard and Libet, 2001).

Philosopher John R. Searle (2000a and b) proposed that a voluntary action appears when a conscious "self" acts on the basis of reason and is capable of *initiating* actions. But we found that the "act now" voluntary process is initiated unconsciously. Therefore, a conscious self could not initiate that process. Any reason for action developed by a conscious self would properly belong in the preplanning or choice-making category; we demonstrated experimentally that that kind of process is distinctly different from the final "act now" process. One can, after all, plan and deliberate about an action without ever acting! Searle's philosophically generated models suffer from a failure to take all experimentally known evidence into account. His models are mostly untested and even untestable.

Back to our experiment: An additional important finding was that W preceded the actual movement of the muscle activation by about 150–200 msec (see Fig. 4.3). Also, the actual difference between actual cerebral initiation and conscious will (W) is probably greater than the 400 msec observed here (using the RP). As noted above, an unknown area elsewhere in the brain may be initiating the activity we record as RPII.

What does this mean? First, the process leading to a voluntary act is *initiated* by the brain *unconsciously*, well before the conscious will to act appears. That implies that free will, if it exists, would not initiate a voluntary act.

There are also broad implications for the timing of voluntary acts where speedy initiation is required, as in most sports activities. A tennis player returning a ball served at 100 miles per hour cannot wait to become aware of his decision to act. Responses to sensory signals in sports require complex mental operations to meet each unique event. They are not ordinary reaction times. Even so, professional sports players will tell you that you are "dead" if you consciously think about your moves.

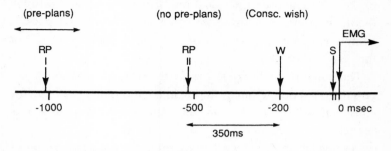

## Self–initiated act: sequence

(pre-plans)            (no pre-plans)    (Consc. wish)

EMG

RP                   RP        W      S

I                   II

-1000           -500      -200      0 msec

350ms

**Fig. 4.3.** Diagram of sequence of events, cerebral (RPs) and subjective (W), that precede a self-initiated voluntary act.

Relative to "O" time (muscle activation), cerebral RPs begin first, either with preplanned acts (RP I) or with no preplannings (RP II). Subjective experience of earliest awareness of the wish to move (W) appears at about −200 msec; this is well before the act ("O" time) but is some 350 msec *after* even RP II. Subjective timings of the skin stimulus (S) averaged about −50 msec, before the actual stimulus delivery time. From Libet, 1989. Reprinted with permission from Cambridge University Press.

### Conscious Veto

The finding that the volitional process is initiated unconsciously leads to the question: Is there then any role for conscious will in the performance of a voluntary act (Libet, 1985)? The conscious will (W) does appear 150 msec *before* the motor act, even though it follows the onset of the cerebral action (RP) by at least 400 msec. That allows it, potentially, to affect or control the final outcome of the volitional process. An interval of 150 msec would allow enough time in which the conscious function might affect the final outcome of the volitional process. (Actually, only 100 msec is available for any such effect. The final 50 msec before a muscle is activated is the time for the primary motor cortex to activate the spinal motor nerve cells, and through them, the muscles. During this final 50 msec, the act goes to completion with no possibility of its being stopped by the rest of the cerebral cortex.)

The conscious will could decide to allow the volitional process to go to completion, resulting in the motor act itself. Or, the conscious will could block or "veto" the process, so that no motor act occurs.

Vetoing of an urge to act is a common experience for all of us. It occurs especially when the projected act is regarded as socially unacceptable, or not in accord with one's overall personality or values. In fact, we showed experimentally that the veto of a planned act was possible even during the last 100–200 msec before the expected time of the action. This was a limited test. It could not be done for a spontaneous veto, as there is then no muscle activation electrically to trigger the computer to record the preceding seconds of the electrical activity of the scalp. So, we were technically limited to study a veto of an act that was planned to be executed at a preset time. The subject was asked to prepare to act at a certain time of the "clock," say at the 10-sec mark. However, the subject was to veto that expected act when the clock reached 100–200 msec before the preset time. A substantial RP developed during the 1–2 actual seconds before the veto, in accord with the subject's report of feeling an expectation to act. But this RP flattened at about 100 to 200 msec before the preset time, as the subject vetoed the act and no muscle response appeared. The observer supplied a trigger signal to the computer at the preset time to act. This at least demonstrated that a person could veto an ex-

when these unconscious processes label an initiative as potentially unacceptable.

## Do We Have Free Will?

The question of free will goes to the root of our views about human nature and how we relate to the universe and natural laws. Are we completely defined by the deterministic nature of physical laws? Are we essentially sophisticated automatons, with our conscious feelings and intentions tacked on as epiphenomena with no causal power? Or, do we have some independence in making choices and actions, not completely determined by known physical laws?

The most common, popular view is that the human individual has a God-given capacity to choose or decide what he wants to do, and that this capacity is not completely subject to deterministic restrictions by the physical laws of nature. Such a view has been promoted by many of the world's religions. Without this view, it becomes difficult to promote an ethics of individual responsibility for one's voluntary actions. The traditional and prevalent view of free will also assumes that a person's will is exercised consciously. When people are completely unaware of their choices for action, and are performing such acts unconsciously, society tends to regard them as having a diminished responsibility for their actions.

Many also believe that God is all-powerful in the control of man and nature. This has produced the related belief that one's "fate" is ordained, and that all of one's activities are beyond the individual's independence. If God knows in advance what you are going to do, then, obviously, your choices for action have been made even before you yourself would have made an independently free decision or choice about an action. (Ironically, the impact of this view of fate and of God's power is the same as that of material determinists, who may be atheists.)

Theologians have, over the centuries, devised different philosophies to permit the existence of free will in a way that is compatible with the view of the universal and all-knowing God. For example, a Jewish mystical sect, the Kabbalists, proposed that God Himself voluntarily relinquished His power to know in advance what human beings will do. That would permit the operation of human free will, a feature that God wanted man to possess (see Cooper, 1997).

### Timing of Brain Processes and Conscious Will

In our experiments, we removed all constraint on freedom of action; subjects performed a simple flick or flexion of the wrist at any time they felt the urge or wish to do so. These voluntary acts were to be performed capriciously, free of any external limitations or restrictions. We have already seen that free will cannot be viewed as an initiator of such a freely voluntary process. We clearly found that the initiation of the preparation to culminate in a freely voluntary movement arises unconsciously in the brain, preceding the conscious awareness of wanting or intending to "act now" by about 400 msec or more.

### Control Function of the Conscious Will

The existence of a veto possibility is not in doubt. The subjects in our experiments at times reported that a conscious wish or urge to act appeared but that they suppressed or vetoed it. In the absence of the muscle's electrical signal when being activated, there was no trigger to initiate the computer's recording of any RP that may have preceded the veto. Thus, there were no recorded RPs with a spontaneously vetoed intention to act. We were, however, able to show that subjects could veto an act planned for performance at a prearranged time. (See the previous section "Conscious Veto").

All of us, not just experimental subjects, have experienced our vetoing a spontaneous urge to perform some act. This often occurs when the urge to act involves some socially unacceptable consequence, like an urge to shout some obscenity at one's professor. Incidentally, in the disorder called Tourette's syndrome, subjects do spontaneously shout obscenities. These acts are actually involuntary. No RP appears before such an act, although an RP does appear before an act voluntarily produced by the Tourette patient. In any person, a quick reaction to an unwarned stimulus also lacks a preceding RP. It is not a conscious freely voluntary act, although it may depend on unconscious processes prepared previously.

As noted above, in addition to a veto, there is another potential function for conscious will. It could serve as a trigger that is required to enable the volitional process to proceed to final action. That would give the conscious will a role in the active production of the motor act. This hypothetical role for conscious will has not been established experimentally. Acts that become somewhat "automatic" can be performed with no reportable conscious wish to do so. But the RP is rather minimal in amplitude and duration before such automatic acts.

Obsessive-compulsive disorder (OCD) provides an interesting and relevant example of an abnormal relation between volitional urges to act and the role of the veto function. In OCD the patient experiences conscious urges to perform a given act repeatedly—like washing the hands over and over again. She clearly lacks the ability to veto each urge, and thus not to act on it. In a fascinating clinical study, the UCLA neurologists J. M. Schwartz and S. Begley (2002) were able to train OCD patients to improve their ability to actively veto the compulsive urge to act. The patients learned to work hard to consciously veto the compulsive process, and thus relieve their OCD. Schwartz and Begley proposed that an active "mental force" had to account for the veto of the compulsive urge to act, and that this conscious mental force could not be explained or accounted for in materialist, determinist views. Recently, a San Francisco psychiatrist told me he has begun to train patients who have tendencies to act violently to veto such violent urges.

All this is in accord with my view of the conscious veto function, and it provides powerful support for my proposal of how free will operates. That is, free will does not *initiate* a volitional process; but it can control the outcome by actively vetoing the volitional process and aborting the act itself, or allowing (or triggering) the act to occur.

In Tourette's syndrome, a condition affecting about 200,000 people in the United States, urges to produce vocal outbursts with often obscene language, as well as other abnormal behaviors, are mostly not consciously controllable. Brain imaging studies (Wolf et al., 1996) have found that the caudate nucleus is involved in this malady. The caudate nucleus is one of the "basal ganglia" located below the cerebral cortex. It appears to be involved in organizing intentional movement behaviors in general. In persons with Tourette's syndrome, the caudate exhibits a heightened sensitivity to dopamine. By contrast, it is a deficiency of the neurotransmitter dopamine that is responsible for Parkinson's disease. Parkinson patients exhibit a lowered ability to initiate a movement (among other motor changes). Interestingly, patients with obsessive compulsive disorder, who find it difficult to suppress (veto) an urge to act, also show an altered activity in the caudate nucleus. These findings raise the possibility that the veto of a volitional urge to act may include a neural action on the caudate nucleus, although it would appear the veto is probably initiated in the prefrontal lobe of the cerebral hemisphere. As noted elsewhere, a lesion in the prefrontal lobe may result in a more uninhibited, often asocial behavior.

In a recent book, the social psychologist Daniel Wegner (2002) presents a lengthy argument for the view that conscious (free) will is an illusion. He accurately describes our experiments showing that voluntary acts are initiated unconsciously by the brain. Wegner, like many others, states that our experimental finding indicates that conscious will "might just be a loose end— one of those things, like the action, that is caused by prior brain" (p. 55) and mental events. However, nowhere in his book does Wegner discuss the veto phenomenon and its provision of a potential causative role for conscious will. That role would be one of controlling the final appearance of a voluntary act, even if the voluntary process is initiated unconsciously before conscious will appears.

### Handling Our Feelings That We Initiate Voluntary Acts

The view, stated in the previous section "Timing of Brain Processes and Conscious Will," of how free will may operate does create a problem: How can we explain our feeling or experience that we initiated an act? If the cerebral process that initiates a freely voluntary act is an unconscious one, the feeling of consciously initiating the process becomes paradoxical. We know that we do become aware of the urge (or wish) to act *before* the actual motor act. That could give rise to the feeling that we had consciously initiated the process. However, the feeling of having initiated the voluntary cannot be valid; we are not aware that the process is actually initiated unconsciously.

On the other hand, it is possible the conscious will, when it appears, acts as a trigger to enable the unconsciously prepared initiative to proceed further to production of the act. In such a case, the conscious feeling of initiating or producing the voluntary act would reflect reality; it would then not be an illusion.

What we are sure of is the ability of the conscious will to block or veto the volitional process and prevent the appearance of any motor act. In other words, conscious free will could control the outcome of an unconsciously initiated process. Whether it has an additional role in enabling a nonvetoed act to proceed to consummation is not presently established experimentally.

### Does the Conscious Veto Have a
### Preceding Unconscious Origin?

We should, at this point, consider the possibility that the conscious veto itself may have its origin in preceding unconscious processes, just as is the case in the development and appearance of the conscious will. If the veto itself were to be initiated and developed unconsciously, the choice to veto would then become an unconscious choice of which we *become* conscious, rather than a consciously causal event. Our own previous evidence showed that the brain "produces" an awareness of something only after about a 0.5-sec period of appropriate neuronal activations (see Chapter 2, and reviews by Libet, 1993, 1996).

Some have proposed that even an unconscious initiation of a veto choice would nevertheless be a genuine choice made by the individual that could still be viewed as a free will process (for example, Velmans, 1991). I find such a proposed view of free will to be unacceptable. In such a view, the individual would not consciously control his actions. He would only become aware of an unconsciously initiated choice. He would have no direct conscious control over the nature of any preceding unconscious processes. But, a free will process implies one can be held consciously responsible for one's choice to act or not to act. We do not hold people responsible for actions performed unconsciously, without the possibility of their conscious control.

For example, actions by a person during a psychomotor epileptic seizure, or by one with Tourette's syndrome (shouting socially abhorrent epithets), are not regarded as actions of free will. Why then should an event unconsciously developed by a normal individual, if it were a process over which he also has no conscious control, be regarded as an act of free will for which he should be held responsible?

I propose, instead, that the conscious veto may not require, or be the direct result of, preceding unconscious processes. The conscious veto is a control function, different from simply becoming *aware* of the wish to act. There is no logical imperative in any mind-brain theory, even in identity theory, that requires specific neural activity to precede and determine the nature of a conscious control function. And there is no experimental evidence against the possibility that the control process may appear without specific development by prior unconscious processes.

Admittedly, to be conscious of the decision to veto does mean one is aware of the event. How may one reconcile this with my proposal? Perhaps we should revisit the concept of awareness, and how it relates to the content of awareness, in cerebral processes that develop both awareness and its contents. Our own previous studies have indicated that awareness is a unique phenomenon in itself, distinguished from the contents of which one may become aware.

For example, awareness of a sensory stimulus can require similar durations of stimulus trains for both somatosensory cortex and for the subcortical pathway (thalamic or medial lemniscus). But the *content* of those awarenesses in these two cases is different; with the cortical stimulus the sensory awareness is subjectively delayed, while it is not subjectively delayed with the stimulus to the subcortical pathway. The content of an unconscious mental process (for example, correct detection of a signal without any awareness of the signal) may be the same as the content (correct detection) when there is awareness of the signal. But to become aware of that same content required that the duration of stimulus to the subcortical pathway be increased by about 400 msec! (See Libet et al., 1991.)

In an endogenous, freely voluntary act, awareness of the intention to act is delayed for about 400 msec after brain processes initiate the process unconsciously (see the previous section "Sequence of Events in the 'Act Now' Situation"). Awareness developed here may be thought of as applying to the whole volitional process. That includes the content of the conscious urge to act and the content of factors that may affect a conscious veto. Awareness of an event may not necessarily be restricted to one detailed item of content in the whole event.

The possibility is not excluded that factors on which the decision to veto is based do develop by unconscious processes that precede the veto. However, the conscious decision to veto could still be made without direct specification for that decision by the preceding unconscious processes. That is, one could consciously accept or reject the program offered up by the whole array of preceding unconscious brain processes. The awareness of the decision to veto could require preceding unconscious processes, but the content of that awareness (the actual decision to veto) is a separate feature that need not have the same requirement.

### What Significance Do Our
### Findings Have for Voluntary Acts?

Can we assume that voluntary acts, other than the simple one studied by us, also have the same temporal relations between unconscious brain processes and the appearance of the conscious wish or will to act? It is common in scientific research to be limited technically to studying a process in a simple system; and then to find that the fundamental behavior discovered with the simple system does indeed represent a phenomenon that appears in other related and more complicated systems. For example, the charge on a single electron was measured by Millikan in one isolated system, but it is also valid for electrons in all systems. In fact, RPs have been found by other investigators to precede other more complex volitional acts, such as beginning to speak or to write. Those investigators did not, however, study the time of appearance of the conscious wish to begin such acts. We may, therefore, allow ourselves to consider what general implications may follow from our experimental findings, when viewed as a feature of voluntary acts in general.

We should also distinguish between deliberations about what choice of action to adopt (including preplanning of when to act on such a choice), and the final intention to actually "act now." One may, after all, deliberate all day about a choice but never act. There is no voluntary act in that case. In our experimental studies we found that in some trials subjects engaged in some conscious preplanning of roughly when to act (say, in the next second or so). But even in those cases, the subjects' reported times of the conscious wish to "act now" was about -200 msec. This value was very close to the values reported for fully spontaneous voluntary acts with no preplanning. In all cases, the onset of the unconscious brain process (RPII) for preparing to act was well before the final conscious intention to act now.

These findings indicate that the sequence of the cerebral volitional processes to act now may apply to all volitional acts, whether they are fully spontaneous or have a history of conscious deliberations. That is, regardless of the presence or absence of advance deliberation or planning, the process for acting now arises unconsciously, about 400 msec before the conscious wish to act now appears. The "act now" process appears to be independent of and separate from the deliberative and planning processes.

### Ethical Implications of How Free Will Operates

The role of conscious free will would be, then, not to initiate a voluntary process (although it may possibly enable the process to finally lead to action). However, conscious will definitely can control whether the act takes place. We may view the unconscious initiatives for voluntary actions as "burbling up" unconsciously in the brain. The conscious will then selects which of these initiatives may go forward to an action, or which ones to veto and abort so no act occurs.

This kind of role for free will is actually in accord with commonly held religious and ethical strictures. Most religious philosophies hold individuals responsible for their actions and advocate that you "control your actions." Most of the Ten Commandments are "do not" orders. The philosopher and religious sage Maimonides "defined holiness as disciplined self-control, as the ability to say no to one's most instinctive physical desires" (as quoted in Rabbi Shlomo Riskin, 1999). In this connection there is an interesting difference between the Jewish and Christian versions of the Golden Rule. Rabbi Hillel, who lived shortly before the era of Jesus, stated it as: "Do *not do* to others what you would *not* have them do to you." In other words, leave other people alone, with tolerance. The Christian view takes a positive, activist view: "*Do* unto others what you would have them *do* unto you." The late philosopher Walter Kaufmann argued that this difference is highly significant in his book *Faith of a Heretic* (1961); Kaufmann noted that, among other things, the Christian Golden Rule could result in actions being imposed on others that run counter to the wishes of others.

### When May One Be Guilty or Sinful?

How do our findings relate to the question of when one may be regarded as guilty or sinful, in various religious and philosophical systems? If we experience a conscious wish or urge to perform a socially unacceptable act, should that be regarded as a sinful event, even if the urge has been vetoed and no act has occurred? Some religious systems answer "yes." President Jimmy Carter admitted to having "a lust in his heart" for some women. Although he did not act on this, he apparently still felt sinful for having experienced a lustful urge. (President Carter was drawing on a Christian tradition deriving from the following two verses in the Sermon on the Mount: [Jesus said], "ye have heard that it was said by them of old time, Thou shalt not commit adultery: But I say unto you, that whosoever looketh on a woman to lust after her hath committed adultery with her already in his heart" (Matthew 5:27–28, recalled for me by Rev. Anthony Freeman).

But any such urges would be initiated and developed in the brain unconsciously, according to our findings. The unconscious appearance of an intention to act could not be controlled consciously. Only its final consummation in a motor act could be consciously controlled. Therefore, a religious system that castigates an individual for simply having a mental intention or impulse to do something unacceptable, even when this is not acted out, would create a physiologically insurmountable moral and psychological difficulty.

Indeed, insistence on regarding an unacceptable urge to act as sinful, even when no act ensues, would make virtually all individuals sinners. The mechanism for the unconscious initiation of such an urge is presumably present in all human beings, and all persons are undoubtedly going to experience socially unacceptable urges and intentions to act. In that sense such a view could provide a physiological basis for original sin! Of course, the concept of original sin could also be based on different views about what is regarded as sinful.

Ethical systems deal with moral codes or conventions that govern how one behaves toward or interacts with other individuals. They are presumably dealing with actions, not simply with urges or intentions. Only an action by one person can directly impinge on the welfare of another. Because it is the *performance* of an act that can be consciously controlled, it should be legitimate to hold individuals guilty of and responsible for their acts.

### Determinism and Free Will

There remains a deeper question about free will that the foregoing considerations have not addressed. What we have achieved experimentally is some knowledge of how free will may operate. But we have not answered the question of (1) whether our consciously willed acts are fully determined by natural laws that govern the activities of nerve cells in the brain, or (2) whether freely voluntary acts, and the conscious decisions to perform them, can proceed to some degree independently of natural determinism. The first of these options would make free will illusory. The conscious feeling of exerting one's will would then be regarded as an epiphenomenon, simply a by-product of the brain's activities with no causal powers of its own.

The view that free will is illusory is elaborated at some length by Wegner (2002). There are, of course, other contributors to this view, like the Churchlands (1999) and Dennett (1984). Wegner proposes a "theory of apparent mental causation" that states: "People experience conscious will when they interpret their own thought as the cause of their action" (p. 64 in his book). That is, the *experience* of conscious will is "quite independent of any actual causal connection between their thoughts and their actions." It is, of course, legitimate to propose this arrangement as a theory for free will within a deterministic view. But there is no crucial evidence that proves its validity. No experimental test has even been proposed in which this theory could be falsified. Without any possibility of falsification, one can propose anything without any fear of being contradicted (as Karl Popper explained).

First, free choices or acts are not predictable, even if they are viewed as completely determined. The "uncertainty principle" of Heisenberg precludes our having a complete knowledge of the underlying molecular activities. Quantum mechanics forces us to deal with probabilities, rather than with certainties of events. And, in chaos theory, a random event may shift the behavior of a whole system in a way that was not predictable. However, even if events are not predictable in practice, that does not exclude the possibility that they are following natural laws and therefore determined.

Let us rephrase our basic question as follows: *Must* we accept determinism? Is nondeterminism a viable option? We should recognize that both of these alternative views (natural law determinism versus nondeterminism) are unproven theories, in other words, unproven in relation to the existence of free will. Determinism (adherence to natural law) has, on the whole, worked well for the physical observable world. That has led many scientists and philosophers to regard any deviation from such determinism as absurd, witless, and unworthy of consideration. But natural laws were derived from observations of physical objects, not from subjective mental phenomena. The latter cannot be directly observed; they are inner experiences of the individual who has them. There has been no evidence, or even a proposed experimental test design, that definitively or convincingly demonstrates the validity of natural law determinism as the mediator or instrument of free choice or free will.

There is an unexplained gap between the category of *physical* phenomena, and the category of *subjective* phenomena. Researchers as far back as Leibniz have pointed out that if you looked into the brain with a full knowledge of its physical makeup and nerve cell activities, you would see nothing that described subjective experience. You would only see cellular structures, their interconnections, and the production of nerve impulses and other electrophysiological events, as well as metabolic chemical changes. The foundation of our own experimental studies of the physiology of conscious experience (beginning in the late 1950s) was that externally observable brain processes and the related reportable subjective introspective experiences must be studied simultaneously, as independent categories, to understand their relationship. The assumption that a deterministic nature of the physically observable world can account for subjective conscious functions and events is a speculative *belief,* not a scientifically proven proposition. (Of course, modern physics teaches us that even physical events may not be determined or predictable. Even so, these physical events are following the natural laws at the macro level. However, that does not exclude the possibility that physical events are susceptible to an external "mental force" at the micro level, in a way that would not be observable or detectable).

Nondeterminism—which is the view that conscious will may, at times, exert effects not in accord with known physical laws— is of course also a nonproven speculative belief. The view that conscious will can affect brain function in violation of known physical laws takes two forms. One view is that the violations are not detectable, because the actions of the mind may be at a level below that of the uncertainty allowed by quantum mechanics. (Whether this last proviso can in fact be tenable is a matter yet to be resolved.) This view would thus allow for a nondeterministic free will to occur without a *perceptible* violation of physical laws. A second view holds that violations of known physical laws are large enough to be detectable, at least in principle. But it can be argued that detectability in actual practice may be impossible. That difficulty for detection would be especially true if the conscious will is able to exert its influence by minimal actions at relatively few nerve elements, if these actions could serve as triggers for amplified nerve cell patterns of activity in the brain. In any case, we do not have a scientific answer to the question of which theory (determinism or nondeterminism) correctly describes the nature of free will.

However, it is important to recognize an almost universal experience: that we can act in certain situations with a free, independent choice and control of whether to act. The simplest example of this is the one we employed in our experimental study—the conscious will to flex the wrist in a freely capricious manner. This provides a kind of *prima facie* evidence that conscious mental processes can causally control some brain processes (Libet, 1993, 1994). Of course, the nature of this experience must be qualified. Our own experimental findings showed that conscious free will does *not initiate* the final "act now" process; the initiation of it occurs unconsciously. But, as discussed previously, conscious will certainly has the potentiality to control the progress and outcome of the volitional process. Thus, the experience of independent choice and of control (of whether and when to act) does have a potentially solid validity as not being an illusion. The cerebral nature of considering *choices* of action, by conscious deliberation and preplanning before any "act now" process, is yet to be elucidated.

How does this experience dovetail with the view of an experimental scientist? It appears to create more difficulty for a determinist than for a nondeterminist option. The phenomenal fact is that most of us feel that we *do* have a kind of free will, at least for some of our actions, within certain limits that may be imposed by our brain's status and by our environment. Our intuitive feelings about the phenomenon of free will form a fundamental basis for our views about human nature. Great care should be taken not to believe allegedly scientific conclusions about our nature that depend on hidden ad hoc assumptions. A theory that simply interprets the phenomenon of free will as illusory and denies the validity of this phenomenal fact is less attractive than a theory that accepts or accommodates the phenomenal fact.

Given that the issue is so fundamentally important to our view of who we are, a claim that our free will is illusory should be based on fairly direct evidence. Theories are supposed to explain observations, not do away with them or distort them, unless there is powerful evidence to justify that. Such evidence is not available, and determinists have not proposed any potential experimental design to test their theory. The elaborate proposals that free will is illusory, like that of Wegner (2002), fall into this category. It is foolish to give up our view of ourselves as having some freedom of action and of not being predetermined robots on the basis of an unproven theory of determinism.

My conclusion about free will, one genuinely free in the non-determined sense, is that its existence is at least as good, if not a better, scientific option than is its denial by natural law determinist theory. Given the speculative nature of both determinist and nondeterminist theories, why not adopt the view that we do have free will (until some real contradictory evidence appears, if it ever does)? Such a view would at least allow us to proceed in a way that accepts and accommodates our own deep feeling that we do have free will. We would not need to view ourselves as machines that act in a manner completely controlled by known physical laws. Such a permissive option has also been recently advocated by the neurobiologist Roger Sperry (see Doty, 1998).

I close, then, with a quotation from the great novelist Isaac Bashevis Singer. Singer stated his strong belief in our having free will. In an interview (Singer, 1968), he volunteered that, "The greatest gift which humanity has received is free choice. It is true that we are limited in our use of free choice. But the little free choice we have is such a great gift and is potentially worth so much that for this itself life is worthwhile living."

# 5

## CONSCIOUS MENTAL FIELD THEORY: EXPLAINING HOW THE MENTAL ARISES FROM THE PHYSICAL

> Present day physics represents a limiting case—valid for inanimate objects. It will have to be replaced by new laws, based on new concepts, if organisms with consciousness are to be described.
>
> —Eugene Wigner, Nobel Laureate, Physics (Quoted by Burns, 1991)

### *What Is the Problem?*

Perhaps the most profound question we can ask is, How can conscious subjective experience arise from activities of nerve cells in the brain? That is, how can the mental arise from the physical? There is no doubt that appropriate neural activities in the human brain are essential for the mental (subjective experience) to appear. Yet, if you were to look into this neural activity and the neuronal structures involved, you would not see anything that looked like subjective experience. Is it possible to attack this profound question experimentally? To attempt that, you would have to recognize that subjective experience cannot be directly measured by external objective devices or by external observations. Conscious subjective experience is accessible only to the individual having the experience. Yet it appears only in relation to appropriate neural activities in the brain. To study it requires an introspective report by an individual describing his experience or awareness of something.

We have seen that the relationship between conscious experience and neuronal activities in the brain can be studied successfully by examining the two features together, as independent but interrelated variables. That is, the neuronal activities and the conscious experience must be observed for the same event, in order to discover which brain activities may signify a conscious experience. Any significance of these for conscious experience would only be established by concomitant studies of conscious experience with brain functions.

However, even a successful investigation of the correlative relationship between conscious experiences and neuronal activities, important as that is, will not answer a more profound problem: How does the categorically different nonphysical phenomenon of subjective experience come from the physical activities of nerve cells? This problem has been termed the "hard problem" by philosopher David Chalmers (1996).

Chalmers (1995) tried to solve this problem by proposing a double-aspect theory of information. He postulated information as having both physical and phenomenal aspects. Experience would emerge from or be identical with the phenomenal aspect. This proposal, which appears to be a version of identity theory, is unconvincing for various reasons (Libet, 1996). Identity theory posits that there is a common "substrate" for all reality, and this substrate has an observable "outer quality" and an "inner quality." The outer quality is what we see and measure as the physical brain; the inner quality of subjective experience is not accessible to an external observer. But identity theory, including the Chalmers's version of it, is not testable; it is therefore not a scientific theory. A different testable solution, the unified conscious mental field, is presented in this chapter.

Philosopher Colin McGinn (1999) views this problem as an "unanswerable question." He sees no conceivable way in which we could account for consciousness and subjective experience in terms of the natural physical order. Spinoza believed he solved the problem by arguing that "thoughts and experiences are always identical with a sequence of objective changes in brain and body." This view suffers from the difficulties with identity theory in general. For one thing, it is not testable, and it does not appear to offer an explanation of how the mental and the physical are causally interactive; it rests on a metaphysical belief, even if an attractive one. I shall attempt to show that it is possible to propose a testable theory as an answer to the problem of the mental and physical.

In addition to Colin McGinn and David Chalmers, several other philosophers are prominent in their writings on the problem of how to relate brain activities to conscious subjective experience. These include John Searle (1992) and Daniel Dennett (1991) along with Paul and Patricia Churchland (1999). The Churchlands represent one extreme in the range of views, that mental subjective phenomena are reducible to physical events in nerve cells. They "advocate a doctrine of eliminative materialism. The view, put baldly, is that mental states do not exist. We *talk* as if they do when we use what has come to be called 'folk psychology'" (see McGinn, 1999, p. 46). That is, we should be content to describe conscious experience in terms of activities of neural circuits. "The mind is a myth," in their view.

On the other hand, Searle (1992) views conscious experience as a real phenomenon, one that is not reducible to the physical activities of the neurons in the brain. That view is, of course, not unique to Searle. My own experimental work since the late 1950s is based on the irreducibility of the two categories of phenomena, the mental and the physical, to each other. McGinn also shares this view, though, like me, he is not in agreement with Searle's further elaborations of this view.

If the Churchlands want to regard themselves as completely determined by the physically materialistic events of nerve cells, they are entitled to their view, even though others feel they have a real conscious mind that is not an automaton. Indeed, it was Descartes in the sixteenth century who asked, What am I really sure of being real? His answer was, It is only my own conscious subjective mind or experience that I am sure is real.

Searle claims that achievement of a complete knowledge of the neural events that are correlated with a conscious experience will tell us all we can know about the mind-brain relationship. Searle views consciousness as simply a biological high-order process of neurons in the brain. McGinn (1999) points out that Searle does not answer the central question of how the biological process of conscious experience results from lower-level physical properties of neurons. What "Searle offers as a solution to the problem is really just a statement of it."

Searle (2000a) went further to present a view of how conscious experience and free action relate to brain function. Searle's model for this view is not in accord with the experimental evidence (Libet, 1985), and it is in fact contradicted by the evidence. For example, Searle states that the conscious "self" is capable of *initiating* a voluntary action. But our experimental findings show that the process to "act now" is initiated unconsciously. Searle's model proposes that "freedom of the will" appears during a "gap" between making a decision to act and the onset of the action process. But the gap is an *unconscious* one of about 400 msec between initiation of the decision and the conscious decision. (See further in my commentary on Searle's proposal, Libet, 2001.) As is the case with many of the philosophers' speculative views on the mind-brain questions, Searle's models have not been tested and are not even testable experimentally.

*The unity of conscious experience* is a phenomenon that is part of the "hard problem." An obvious example lies in our experience of a visual image. The image is based on the activities of thousands of nerve cells. The spatial pattern of these activities, in the primary receiving visual area of cerebral cortex, does not look like the image we see; it is distorted. Other features of the visual image are represented or developed in other cortical visual areas; these are specialized for color vision, motion of an image, recognition of faces, and so on. In spite of this complex array of separable neural functions, we see subjectively a unified image, with all of these visual elements smoothly integrated. This is only one small example of our unified, integrated experience arising from complex patterns of nerve cell activities.

Still another feature of the hard problem is the question of how free will operates. If free will is accepted as a valid phenomenon, a conscious mental function (presumably nonphysical) is needed to influence the activities of physical nerve cells. This problem is the converse of the question of how physical nerve cells can give rise to conscious subjective experience.

Indeed, "five mysteries of the mind" have been elegantly put forth by Doty (1998).

### How Do Emergent Phenomena Relate to the Problem?

In the physical world we recognize that the phenomena displayed by a system may not be evident in the properties of the subunits that make up that system. For example, the compound benzene is composed of six carbon and six hydrogen atoms. Kekulé proposed that the six carbon atoms are connected in a ring structure, with the hydrogens bound to the ring at the six junctions between the six carbon atoms in the ring. This is the famous benzene ring fundamental to organic chemistry (and to biology). The properties exhibited by benzene (as an organic solvent and so on) could not have been predicted, *a priori*, from the properties of the carbon and hydrogen atoms themselves. That is, a new property emerged from the $C_6H_6$ ring system. Similarly, the properties of a wheel are not evident from the properties of the materials used to construct the wheel (as noted by Sperry, 1980). The wheel's property of rolling emerges from the system created by the specific arrangement of the materials used to make the wheel. The appearance of a magnetic field around a wire that is conducting an electric current is also a phenomenon that emerges in that system. As the astrophysicist Sir Arthur Eddington once said, "We used to believe that if we knew one thing and then another, then we know two, because one and one are two. We are now discovering that we must learn more about the 'and'" (quoted by B. D. Josephson, 1993). In other words, there are properties of systems that are not evident in its component parts.

We are virtually forced to regard conscious subjective experience similarly, as a phenomenon that somehow emerges from an appropriate system of activities of the physical nerve cells in the brain. However, unlike physical emergent phenomena, the emergent subjective experience is not directly observable or measurable by any physical means, as subjective experience is only accessible to the individual having the experience. Clearly, the emergent subjective experience of this system is unlike the properties of the responsible nerve cells; it could not have been a predicted outcome of these neural activities. It should not be surprising that the emergent subjective experience exhibits unique unexpected characteristics.

Why subjective experience emerges from appropriate neuronal activities may be no more answerable than similar questions about other fundamental phenomena. That is, why does mass have inertia? Why do masses exhibit gravitational attraction? Why does matter behave both in wave-like and quantal fashions? Fundamental physical phenomena are not reducible or explainable. We simply accept these as "given" in the nature of things. We can only study how these manifestations affect, interact, and control what goes on in the physical world.

We may thus regard conscious, subjective experience as another unique fundamental property in nature. What are some of its unique characteristics, *in addition to* subjective experience or awareness itself? These are the unity of subjective experience and the potentiality for influencing nerve cell activities. These characteristics are also not evident in the neuronal substrate from which subjective experience emerges.

### How to Deal with the Unity of Conscious Subjective Experience

One of the most mysterious and seemingly intractable problems in the mind-brain relationship is that of the unitary and integrated nature of conscious experience. We have a brain with an estimated 100 billion neurons, each of which may have thousands of interconnections with other neurons. It is increasingly evident that many functions of cerebral cortex are localized. This is not merely true of the primary sensory areas for each sensory modality, of the motor areas that command movement, and of the speech and language areas—all of which have been known for some time. Many other functions now find localized representations, including visual interpretations of color, shape, and velocity of images; recognition of human faces; and preparation for motor actions. Localized function appears to extend even to the microscopic level within any given area. The cerebral cortex appears to be organized into functional and anatomical vertical columns of cells, each a millimeter or so in width. There are discrete interconnections within the column and with other columns near and far, as well as with selective subcortical structures. This columnar view began with findings by Mountcastle (1957) and has been greatly extended by him and others. For example, there are the columnar localizations of visual shapes and motions and of binocular vision, as discovered by Hubel and Wiesel (1962).

In spite of the enormously complex array of localized functions and representations, the conscious experiences related to or elicited by these neuronal features have an integrated and unified nature. For example, we subjectively see a smoothly unified image when we look at any objects or environmental pattern, even though the cerebral representation of that image is *not* similarly unified. Whatever does reach awareness is not experienced as an infinitely detailed array of widely individual events. It may be argued that this amazing discrepancy between particularlized neuronal representations and unitary integrated conscious experience should simply be accepted as part of a general lack of isomorphism between mental and neural events. But that just applies some verbal names to the phenomenon. It avoids the profound question of how that mismatch leads to unified experience. One would not like to exclude the possibility that some unifying process or phenomenon may mediate the profound transformation in question.

The general problem of subjective unity in the face of physical disunity has been recognized by many others, going back at least to a founder of modern neurophysiology, Sherrington (1940), and probably earlier. Eccles (in Popper and Eccles, 1977, p. 362) proposed that "the experienced unity comes not from a neurophysiological synthesis but from the proposed integrating character of the self-conscious mind." He made this proposal in conjunction with a dualist-interactionist view in which a separate nonmaterial mind could detect and integrate the neuronal activities. Some more monistically inclined neuroscientists have also been arriving at related views (for example, Sperry, 1952, 1980; Doty 1984)—in other words, integration seems to be best accountable for in the mental sphere that emerges from the neuronal activities.

There has been a growing consensus that no single cell or group of cells is likely to be the site of a conscious experience, but rather that conscious experience is an attribute of a more global or distributed function of the brain (for example, see

Edelman and Mountcastle, 1978; Baars, 1989). But not all cell groups in the brain are involved in producing awareness. We have shown experimentally that not all nerve cell activities give rise to a conscious experience (Libet, 1973, 1985; Libet et al., 1991). For example, a *short* train (say of 100-msec duration) of stimulus pulses to sensory cortex elicits responses of many nerve cells without any subjective experience.

More recently, a widespread synchronization of oscillatory neuronal responses to certain visual configurations was discovered (Gray and Singer, 1989; Singer, 1991, 1993). Singer concluded that their results "provide experimental support for a central postulate of Edelman's group selection theory." These results led to some speculation that a "correlation" model might represent the neural coding for recognizing a unified image in an otherwise chaotic background. That is, the synchronous correlation of electrical oscillations would give a unified subjective image. This speculation is still to be tested directly. But even if a proper correlation between synchronization of neurons and a unified subjective experience were to be found, that would not explain why the subjective experience is unified in a complete manner and with no gaps in the spatial and colored image, unlike the synchronized activities of separate groups of nerve cells.

### How Does Free Will Arise?

Another apparently intractable problem in the mind-brain relationship is the question of whether the interaction between the mind and the brain can go in both directions. There is no doubt that cerebral events or processes can influence, control, and presumably "produce" mental events, including conscious ones. The reverse of this principle, that mental processes can influence or control neuronal ones, has been generally unacceptable to many scientists on (often unexpressed) philosophical grounds. Yet our own feelings of conscious control of at least some of our behavioral actions and mental operations would seem to provide *prima facie* evidence for such a reverse interaction.

This reverse feature is obviously fundamental to the issue of free will (see Chapter 4). There have been many views proposed historically about mind influencing brain, mostly from theologians and philosophers. These have had important and provocative effects on the general populations of the world. However, they are virtually all not testable by objective or scientific criteria.

Even the serious and detailed theses proposed by neuroscientists have been speculative solutions that are thought-provoking but are not experimentally testable. Sir John Eccles (1990), a Nobel laureate in neurobiology, proposed a dualistic solution. He proposed that mental units (called psychons) are separate from nerve cells but can affect the probability of release of the chemical transmitter substance at synaptic junctions. Such a power could then influence the ability of a given nerve cell to deliver a message to the next cell in its network. Roger Sperry (1980), the Nobel laureate who established that the right and left sides of the brain could function differently and even independently, argued for a monistic solution that did not separate the mental and physical attributes of brain function. Sperry proposed that mental activity emerges from the physical system, the brain. But the emergent mental activity could, in turn, influence neuronal activity in the brain. He limited that influence to "supervening" but not "intervening" in neuronal activity. That limitation allowed Sperry to remain a determinist in his view. However, after struggling for decades with the problem of how to accommodate a humanistic free-will aspect of human beings with a deterministic view, Sperry finally abandoned strict determinism. He opted for the possibility that mental functions may actually control some neuronal activities in a manner not completely governed by the natural laws of the physical world (see Doty, 1998). Unfortunately, both these views (of Eccles and Sperry) remain philosophical theories having explanatory power but without experimentally testable formats.

## Does a Unified Conscious Mental Field Provide a Solution?

As one possible experimentally testable solution to both features of the mind-brain relationship, I have proposed that we may view conscious subjective experience as if it were a *field*, produced by appropriate though multifarious neuronal activities of the brain (Libet, 1993, 1994). Such a field would provide communication within the cerebral cortex without the neural connections and pathways in the cortex.

A conscious mental field (CMF) would provide the mediator between the physical activities of nerve cells and the emergence of subjective experience. It thus offers an answer to the profound question of the nonphysical mental arising from the physical.

A chief quality or attribute of CMF would be that of a unified or unitary subjective experience. That is, the CMF would be the entity in which unified subjective experience is present. A second attribute would be a causal ability to affect or alter some neuronal functions. The additional meaning or explanatory power of describing subjective experience in terms of a CMF will become more evident with the proposed experimental testing of the theory. That is, the CMF is proposed as more than just another term for referring to "unified subjective experience."

The putative CMF would *not* be in any category of known physical fields, such as electromagnetic, gravitational, and so on. The conscious mental field would be in a phenomenologically independent category; it is not describable in terms of any externally observable physical events or of any known physical theory as presently constituted. In the same sense as for all subjective events, the CMF would be detectable only in terms of subjective experience, accessible only to the individual who has the experience. An external observer could only gain valid direct evidence about the conscious mental field from an introspective report by the individual subject. In this respect the conscious mental field would differ from all known physical fields whose existence and characteristics are amenable to physical observations. The CMF theory may be viewed as an extension of Roger Sperry's theory of "the mental" as an emergent property of "the physical" brain.

The proposed CMF should be viewed as an operational phenomenon, in other words, as a working and testable feature of brain function. You may think of the CMF as somewhat analogous to known physical force fields (Libet, 1997, following Popper et al., 1993). For example, a magnetic field is produced by electric current flowing in a conductor, but it can in turn influence the flow of the current. However, as indicated, the CMF cannot be observed directly by external physical means.

How is the CMF attribute of unified subjective experience related to its production by contributions from local neuronal areas? Local alterations in the CMF would be reflected in a changed overall field, but there would not be a separately required mechanism for transmission and integration of such local contributions. To think in terms of a transmission and integrative process would be to continue thinking in terms of the externally observable neural events. To do so would be a misunderstanding of the nature of the proposed CMF, which is in a phenomenological category not reducible to (although intimately related with) neuronal processes. There are no doubt rules for (at least much of) the relationship between the CMF and the physically (externally) observable neural processes. But the rules are not describable *a priori*—in other words, before they are discovered by studying both phenomena simultaneously (see Libet, 1987, 1989).

In the split-brain studies of Sperry et al. (1969; Sperry, 1985), the main communicating commissures, the large bundles of nerve fibers connecting the two cerebral hemispheres, were transected, or cut through. Neurosurgeons do that to control epileptic seizures that bounce back and forth between the two cerebral hemispheres. The researchers then found that there can be simultaneously different contents of experience for the two sides. Normally the two hemispheres talk to each other by means of the large commissures and they share the same information. With the commissures split, however, the new contents of mental events in the right hemisphere are not available to the left hemisphere, and vice versa. As a result, any contributions of right hemisphere activity to a mental field presumably cannot directly alter a CMF of the left hemisphere. Unity of the CMF would, in these circumstances, be restricted to a given hemisphere. In addition, contributions of local neural areas to the overall CMF of a hemisphere would only be effective when contiguous with those of other areas; in other words, the contributions would not be effective across substantial gaps of space or of tissue barriers, of the dimensions present between the two hemispheres. If the CMF cannot cross a barrier between the two adjacent hemispheres, it clearly cannot provide a basis for messages to be transmitted to or received from another person's brain. There is no provision for mental telepathy in the CMF theory. Sperry (1984) had previously pointed out that the split-brain phenomena argue against any mental telepathy between persons, if one hemisphere cannot communicate with the adjacent hemisphere in the absence of the major interconnecting nerve bundles (see also Buser, 1998).

Incidentally, these features raise other fundamental questions: Is the right hemisphere conscious? Are there two selves in one individual, one self in each hemisphere?

The right hemisphere does appear to be capable of being conscious, even though it has a very limited ability to speak. I had an opportunity to see a video of a patient from whom the left hemisphere had been surgically removed due to its pathology. The excision was done when the patient was an adult. That obviated the possible adjustments that can occur in the right hemisphere when the left hemisphere is removed or otherwise absent in childhood. This adult patient behaved as if he were conscious. He looked alert; he responded to questions in a proper manner. At times, because he was not able to answer by speaking, he showed he was frustrated and disgusted by this limitation.

The question of two selves is a more complicated one (see Bogen, 1986; Doty, 1999). Split-brain patients do not report disturbances of their feelings as a unified person. That is, they feel like the same single person they were before the surgical split. When not being tested with inputs restricted to one hemisphere, both hemispheres can receive the same sensory information. These patients' eyes can roam about over all the same visual fields. Still, it is quite remarkable that they do not report feeling that there is a partner conscious agent; they feel they are still one self.

We may postulate that some aspect of the putative CMF can,

in fact, bridge both hemispheres. Or, there may be neural cross-overs at lower levels of the brain, below the cerebral hemispheres, that could somehow account for the unified personality.

### Is There an Experimental Design to Test the CMF Theory?

Any scientific theory, especially one like the CMF, must be testable to be taken seriously. The theory of a CMF makes crucial predictions that can, at least in principle, be tested experimentally. If local areas of cerebral cortex can independently contribute to or alter the larger, unitary CMF, it should be possible to demonstrate such contributions when (1) the cortical area is completely isolated or cut off from all neuronal communication with the rest of the brain; but (2) the area remains *in situ*, alive and kept functioning in some suitable manner that sufficiently resembles its normal behavior. The experimental prediction to be tested would be as follows: Suitable electrical or chemical activation of the isolated tissue should produce or affect a conscious experience even though the tissue has no neural connections to the rest of the brain. Communication would then have to take place in the form of some field that does not depend on nerve pathways.

The researchers would have to control for the possibilities of spread of influences from the isolated block via physical non-neural paths (for example, electric current flow). If a subjective experience were induced and reported within a second or so, that would tend to exclude spread by chemical diffusion as well as by changes in vascular circulation or in contents of circulating blood (see Ingvar, 1955).

Suitable neuronal isolation could be achieved either (1) by

surgically cutting all connections to the rest of the brain, but leaving sufficient vascular connections and circulation intact, or (2) by temporarily blocking all nerve conduction into and out of an area. Surgical isolation is discussed further later in this chapter.

Functional isolation might be achievable by injecting blocking agents in small amounts to form a ring of blockade around and under a selected block of cerebral cortex. A local anesthetic agent might be used, such as procaine suitably buffered to pH 7.4 in Ringer's solution. Or tetrodotoxin, the selective blocker of sodium-conducted action potentials, could be combined with a calcium-channel blocker like verapamil (to ensure that calcium-mediated action potentials did not escape blockade). The advantage of this pharmacological method for isolation is its reversibility, which means it could be used on areas of cortex not scheduled for surgical excision, thus greatly enlarging the pool of potential subjects (if risk factors are suitably met). The disadvantages of this method are (1) the difficulty of limiting the blockade to a narrow band around the slab, because of diffusibility; (2) the need to prove that complete blockade has been achieved; and (3) a reduced ability to introduce neural inputs into the isolated slab, by the excitation of ascending nerve fibers within the slab but near its lower borders. The chemical blockade would inactivate some portion of these nerve fibers by local diffusion.

### How Can a Surgically Isolated Slab of Cerebral Cortex Be Produced in situ?

A slab of cerebral cortex can be neurally isolated surgically. By making all of the cuts subpially, the blood supply to the cortex is not interrupted; it remains as the only connection of the isolated slab with the rest of the brain. The cortical slab remains in place and viable. The pia arachnoid is the thin membrane in direct contact with the surface of the brain, including the cerebral cortex. The blood vessels to the cortex travel horizontally in the pial membrane. At separate points a branch of blood vessels dips down vertically into the cortex. Cuts of the cortex can be made just below the pia, leaving the blood vessels intact.

Studies of the electrophysiological activity of such isolated cortex *in situ* have been reported (Kristiansen and Courtois, 1949; Burns, 1951, 1954; Echlin et al., 1952; Ingvar, 1955; Goldring et al., 1961). The basic method involved introducing a narrow curved blade through an opening in an avascular area of the pia arachnoid membrane. The surgeon would undercut a block or slab of cortex and, by bringing the tip of the curved blade up to meet the pia at some distance away and rotating the tip in a circle, he would also cut the connections to adjacent cortex.

In an earlier study (of how vertical cuts in the connections between adjacent cortical areas might affect the integrated, organized function of the sensorimotor cortex in monkeys), Sperry (1947) used a somewhat different technique (Fig. 5.1). The cutting instrument was an extremely thin double-edged blade made from a fine wire or sewing needle. The sharpened end portion of this wire was bent to a right angle; this terminal portion of the blade was sunk vertically into the cortex so its horizontal arm lay just below the pia. When the vertical knife was pushed forward it cut through the cortex while its horizontal carrying arm slid just below the pia. This technique could easily be arranged to produce undercutting of the cortex as well. The advantage of Sperry's method lies in the very thin line of tissue damage created by this knife, which produces chronic scars less

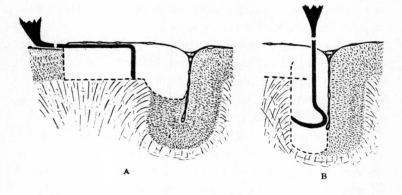

A                               B

**Fig. 5.1.** Production of a viable isolated slab of cerebral cortex.

A. A fine wire is bent into the shape as shown. The leading vertical arm is sharpened before insertion into the cortex. The vertical leading edge is inserted into the cortex to a depth at which its horizontal arm is just below the surface (pia arachnoid) membrane. Pushing the vertical arm forward now cuts off that side of the cortex from adjacent connections. By cutting all sides and then arranging the knife to undercut the slab, that piece of cortex becomes completely disconnected from all neural connections with the rest of the brain, but it remains alive because it retains its blood supply from vessels in the surface membrane.

B. Shows a related shape of the knife used to cut down into the cortical gyrus that borders the sulcus (space) next to the adjacent gyrus.

From Sperry, 1947. With permission from the American Physiological Society.

than 100 $\mu$m thick. That is particularly desirable if the surgeon plans to leave the isolated slab *in situ* for therapeutic reasons. When a piece of cortex must be excised to remove an intractable epileptic focus, simply isolating the offending focal tissue in the manner described here appears advantageous. That approach avoids the growth of dangerous scar tissue that tends to occur in a cavity produced by removal of the focal cortex. In recent years, many neurosurgeons have adopted the isolation technique, which was introduced by Morrell.

Echlin et al. (1952) isolated a cortical slab in human subjects with both general and local anesthesia (patient awake). They reported an immediate reduction but not complete abolition of rhythmic electrical activity (EEG) in the isolated area. After 20 minutes, paroxysmal bursts of high-voltage activity appeared. This kind of seizure pattern in a normal brain is usually associated with disruption or distortion of normal functions and, in the motor area, convulsive motor actions. There was no spread of activity from the isolated slab to surrounding areas.

The physiological properties of the cortical slab are obviously immediately altered when it is isolated, because of the sudden loss of all neural inputs. For example, it is well known that destruction of the reticular activating system in the brain stem, which ascends to end diffusely in the cerebral cortex, results in a coma. This afferent input would have to be properly replaced so as to "wake up" the isolated slab of cortex. Procedures to restore some levels of sufficiently normal activity would be necessary. The nerve fiber inputs from below, and their synaptic contacts with cells in the slab, would degenerate some hours after the cuts separated them from their cells of origin to produce isolation. Therefore the studies proposed in my experimental design (to test for the CMF) need to be carried out in the acute phase, during the initial period after isolation. With the afferent cut axons still viable and potentially functional, they could be used to restore some degree of neural inputs to the nerve cells in the slab. These ascending nerve fibers could be electrically excited by the surgeon inserting fine stimulating electrodes to reach the lower levels of the isolated slab. Electrical recordings of activity at the surface of the slab could serve as indicators that the isolated slab has returned to some "awake" normal condition.

*How to find the proper patient and tissue?* Surgical isolation of a slab of cortical tissue would, of course, result in a permanent loss of its normal neuronal functions. As a result, studies are limited to patients in whom a slab of cortical tissue has been therapeutically designated for surgical removal. The procedure would be carried out in the operating room before the excision of the tissue, if other conditions were also met. The patient would have to be awake and responsive; the surgeon would have to use local rather than general anesthesia to produce the cortical exposure; the patient would have to provide informed consent and be cooperative; and risk assessments would have to be approved by all concerned, particularly the hospital or university committee for protection of human subjects. Many patients have tolerated brain surgery under local anesthesia and have participated fruitfully in past studies (for example, Penfield, 1958; Libet et al., 1964; Libet, 1973). In such procedures, it is desirable for the neurosurgeon to include a bit of fairly normal responding tissue within the slab scheduled for excision; luckily, neurosurgeons almost always include such normal bits to achieve an adequately therapeutic removal of pathological tissue.

There is a further requirement for this experiment. Electrical stimulation of the cerebral cortex elicits a reportable conscious experience only at very limited sites. The most effective of these sites are the primary sensory areas, which receive the specifically localized sensory messages. There is a primary sensory area for body sensations (in the postcentral gyrus of cortex), for vision (in the so-called striate cortex of the occipital lobe), and for audition (in the upper lip of the temporal lobe). Stimulation elsewhere does excite nerve cells, but the responses do not lead to activation of a system that can produce a reportable conscious experience. Because the testing tool is electrical stimulation of the cortex, the researcher had better do that on an area at which such stimulation normally elicits an introspective report of an experience.

Very few patients—five to ten worldwide each year—meet this requirement. Even when patients have an epileptic focus in a primary sensory area, surgeons are very reluctant to cut out that focus, as the patients then may suffer a serious loss of sensation. To find a cooperative neurosurgeon with access to such patients has proved to be a daunting process.

## Can the CMF Influence Nerve Cell Activity?

A test of the causal ability of the putative CMF to affect neuronal functions is already implicit in the test just described for the existence of the CMF. If stimulation of the isolated cortical slab can elicit an introspective report by the subject, the CMF must be able to activate the appropriate cerebral areas required to produce the verbal report.

The proposed experiment, using an isolated but living slab of cerebral cortex, could provide a direct answer to the question of whether a CMF could affect nerve cell functions in a way that accounts for the role of conscious will.

Other proposals for the possible actions of the conscious will are subject to ambiguity in interpretation. For example, neural activity (as indicated by measurements of regional blood flow or metabolic rate) has been shown to increase selectively in the supplementary motor area (SMA) when a subject is asked to imagine moving her fingers without actually moving them (Ingvar and Phillipson, 1977; Roland and Friberg, 1985). Eccles has taken this to be a demonstration of a mental action (imagination of moving) that can affect neural activities. But there are difficulties with such a conclusion from that experiment. The indications of an increase in neuronal activity by the imaging methods, whether PET scan or MRI, are based on an increase in local blood flow or metabolism. But such increases in blood flow or metabolism appear only after a substantial delay, probably seconds, following any actual change in local nerve cell activity. The delay obscures the determination of the relative timing of the mental imaging and the increase in local nerve cell activity. Additionally, there is always the possibility that the whole process was initiated by some neural events elsewhere in the brain, too small or oriented so they are not recorded by the imaging method. Unless the mental event (of imagining or command) could be shown to precede *any* possible neural event specifically related to the process studied, there would always be doubt about the nature of the causal interaction. With the neurally isolated cortical slab, there are no such difficulties of interpretation.

## General Conclusions on CMF Theory

Suppose that the experimental results prove to be positive; in other words, suitable stimulation of the neurally isolated cortex elicits some reportable subjective response that is not attributable to stimulation of adjacent nonisolated cortex or of other cerebral structures. That would mean that activation of a cortical area can contribute to overall unified conscious experience by some mode other than by neural messages delivered via nerve conduction. This result would provide crucial support for the proposed field theory, in which a cortical area can contribute to or affect the larger conscious field. It would provide an experimental basis for a unified field of subjective experience and for mental intervention in neuronal functions.

With such a finding, you might ask, What would be the role of all the massive and complex neural interconnections, cortico-cortical, cortical-subcortical, and hemisphere to hemisphere? And here is a possible answer: to subserve all the cerebral functions other than those directly related to the appearance of the conscious subjective experience and its role in conscious will. It should be noted that all cognitive functions (receipt, analysis, recognition of signals), information storage, learning and memory, processes of arousal and attention and of states of affect and mood, and so on) are *not* proposed as functions to be organized or mediated by the postulated CMF (conscious mental field). In short, it is *only the phenomenon of conscious subjective experience,* associated with all the complex cerebral functions, that is modeled in the CMF, in an admittedly speculative manner.

Some may easily dismiss the prospect of obtaining positive results in the proposed experimental tests, because such results would be completely unexpected from prevalent views of brain functions based on physical connectivities and interactions. But the improbability of positive results is strictly a function of existing views that do not deal successfully with the problems of unity of subjective experience and of apparent mental controls of brain processes. The potential implications of the CMF theory and of the positive results it predicts are clearly profound in nature. On those grounds, and because the proposed experiments are in principle workable though difficult, the proposed experimental design should merit a serious place in investigations of the mind-brain problem.

As the theoretical physicist Niels Bohr once said about a new theory, "When the great innovation appears, it will seem muddled and strange. It will only be half understood by its discoverer and a mystery to everyone else. For any idea that does not appear bizarre at first, there is no hope" (quoted by Mukhopadhyay, 1995).

## Does the CMF Mean Dualism?

The essential feature in the dualist view is the proposal that the physical and the mental phenomena represent two separable entities. The extreme version of dualism was that from Descartes. He proposed that there are two kinds of substances: res cogitans, which exhibits mental and conscious properties; and res extensa, the substance of the physical world (including the person's body). He claimed that the two substances communicated with each other by way of the pineal gland. The pineal gland is the only brain structure that is single; all other brain structures are bilateral and thus doubled. Descartes thought the single pineal gland could thus account for the unitary nature of consciousness. A major distinction for Descartes was that the mental is nondivisible and unitary, while the physical world is divisible and has extension (in other words, location in space).

But there are less extreme versions of dualism. These do not postulate separable substances. Rather, they propose there is some kind of dualistic aspect in the relationship between the physical and mental worlds, which proponents claim accounts for the apparent nonreducibility between the two worlds. That is, mental subjective phenomena cannot *a priori* be described by any knowledge of physical events and structures; and, conversely, physical events (including the neuronal ones in the brain) cannot be described by knowledge of the accompanying mental subjective events. Only the correlative relationship between the two categories of events can be studied and described.

This view does not require the existence of separate kinds of substances. In identity theory, the mental and the physical phenomena are regarded as two aspects of a unitary substrate; this is a "dual aspect" theory. There is an "inner" aspect, the subjective, accessible only to the individual, and an "outer" or "external" aspect, represented in the externally observable physical structures and functions of the brain. This theory seems untestable because there is no way of getting directly at the unitary substrate that allegedly exhibits this double aspect. Identity theory is actually proposed as a "monist," not a dualist theory; but the definitions of monism versus dualism begin to lose their usefulness at these levels. (Remember that definitions are constructs designed to be helpful when considering different phenomena; when they cease to be helpful, you should abandon them, at least for those conditions.)

So, how does the CMF fit into this argument? The CMF is proposed as a "property" of an emergent phenomenon of the brain. The CMF is clearly not in the separate substance category of Cartesian dualism. The CMF does not exist without the brain. It emerges from the appropriate system of neural activities.

On the other hand, the emergent CMF phenomenon is postulated to exhibit qualities not describable by the physical brain's activities that gave rise to the CMF. In a sense, that is analogous to conditions in the physical world, in which the properties of a system are not describable by those of the components that make up the system. (See the example I provided earlier of benzene, the system produced by six carbon and six hydrogen atoms.) The major difference from all other systems is that the CMF is not directly observable by physical measurements. The attributes of the CMF are only accessible to the individual whose brain has generated that particular CMF. If you want to call this situation dualistic, you should realize that this kind of dualism is not Cartesian; in a sense, it also applies to all physical systems.

A charge leveled at any form of dualism has been that it puts a "ghost in the machine" (see Ryle, quoted in McGinn, 1997). The machine is the brain and the ghost is the mental conscious phenomenon because it is not physically observable. I have, of course, argued the latter is true of conscious subjective experience, whether or not it is involved as an attribute of a CMF. It is a fact that subjective experience is not evident in or describable by purely physical observations of nerve cell activities. Correlations between the subjective and the physical must be discovered by simultaneous studies of both categories.

You can, of course, ask the proponents of the "anti-ghost" argument, How do they know there is no ghost in the machine? The answer is that they do not really know. The emergence of conscious subjective experience from nerve cell activities is still a mystery. If you want to refer to subjective experience as a ghost, you can do so. This anti-ghost belief reminds me of an analogous argument between Einstein and Stephen Hawking (1988). Einstein disliked the proposal in quantum theory that events are probabilistic rather than certain. Einstein said he did not believe God played dice with the universe. Hawking's response was, "How does Einstein *know* that God does not play dice with the universe?"

There is another argument against mental, subjective functions that are not predictable from knowledge of the physical system. Such a mind would be a loose cannon, with chaotic properties not strictly tied to observable brain functions. But that description presumes that such a mind would not have its own constraints, even if these were not describable or predictable from the physical observations of the cerebral system from which this mind would emerge. Second, mental functions often do empirically operate like a loose cannon. As a result, the loose cannon argument is not necessarily contradictory to a partially indeterminate mind.

Regardless of whether the CMF theory is valid, a knowledge of nerve cell structures and functions can never, in itself, explain or describe conscious subjective experience. As noted earlier, studying the brain can show you what nerve cells are doing and so forth, but there is nothing in that which exhibits or describes any subjective experience. Also, it is possible that some mental phenomena have no direct neuronal basis (see Chapter 3) and it is also possible that the conscious will does not always obey the natural laws of the physical world (see Chapter 4).

We may, therefore, have to be satisfied with knowledge of how conscious subjective experience is related to brain activities, but we may not be able to explain why or how subjective experience can be produced by brain activities any more than we can explain why gravity is a property of matter. We accept that each fundamental category of phenomena exists and that its relation to other systems may be studied without knowing why such relationships exist.

# 6

## WHAT DOES IT ALL MEAN?

Oh God—Thy ship is so Great, and my boat is so small.

—Anonymous

The work is not yours to finish, but neither are you free
to take no part in it.

—Rabbi Tarfon, in *Ethics of the Fathers* (quoted by Wouk,
1988)

### An Imaginary Dialogue between
### René Descartes and the Author (BL)

René Descartes (1596–1650) is regarded as the pioneer philosopher who attempted to deal with the relation between mind
and body in a systematic manner. An imaginary dialogue with
him may point up how some of our present findings and views
have developed in comparison with the basic views of Descartes
more than 400 years ago.

Descartes started by asking, What am I absolutely sure of?

His answer was: Only of my own existence. He expressed this as "Cogito ergo sum" (I think therefore I am) (see *Treatment of Man,* 1644).

Descartes was a father of the dualist view, in which mind and body (including the brain) represent two separate "substances." He proposed a scheme to explain how the two separate substances could interact and affect each other. These Cartesian views of the mind-body dualism have been subjected to scorn and vilification, especially by modern philosophers, but they cannot be dismissed either logically or on the basis of existing experimental evidence. In any case, Descartes's recognition of the distinctions between mind and the brain, and of the critical role of the brain for the thinking functions, provided a fundamental basis for later developments of how brain and mind may be related.

In addition, Descartes's separation of the body (and external world generally) from any metaphysical properties and from any subjective mental aspects freed physics and physiology to pursue a mechanistic approach. Descartes thus helped to establish a philosophical basis for the development of objective scientific study of the observable world.

In this imaginary dialogue, the responses by Descartes are based, insofar as possible, on the views he expressed in his own writings.

BL: M. Descartes, it is an honor for me to be able to discuss with you some of the topics in the mind-body relationship, in which you were a pioneer. At the present time, I shall try to take into account the increased factual knowledge achieved by the end of the twentieth century, particularly our own experimental findings.

RD: I am happy to have this interchange with you. As you know, I had a reputation for not being tolerant of criticisms of my views, although I did reply to the important criticisms with a detailed analysis. I shall try now to face with a relaxed objectivity the arguments you may raise. I do want to note that my appearance here in your time cannot be regarded as proof of immortality.

BL: You are, of course, well known for your insistence on starting with a basic truth of which one can have no doubts. This was summed up in your pronouncement, "Cogito ergo sum." That is, "I think, therefore, I am." One could doubt whatever one thinks, but about one's thinking there can be no doubt. Or, we cannot doubt our existence without existing while we doubt.

Now, you have been accused of emphasizing rational thought as perhaps the real feature of the thinking mind. In fact, there is a recent book by an eminent neuro-psychologist, Antonio Damasio (1994), with the title *Descartes's Error: Emotion, Reason and the Human Brain*. Damasio argues that emotional feelings are the primary engine of the mind, rather than rational thinking. Could you clarify for us what you really meant by "thinking"?

RD: Mais oui. It is true that I emphasized rational thinking as a supreme judge of truth, but only in relation to the abstract sciences like mathematics. However, I defined my concept of "thinking" much more broadly in several places in my writings.

I regarded thought as meaning all that we are immediately conscious of. That includes being conscious of our will, intellect, imagination, senses, emotional feelings, our loves, hates, desires, joy, sadness, anger, and so on.

(See my *Philosophical Works* and also my *Meditations* in Descartes, 1644.) I specifically wrote that emotional feelings or passions can affect the actions of our conscious mind. So, the distinction between my views and those of Damasio is not a black-and-white one; rather, it is perhaps a difference in the emphasis on the role of emotions.

BL: In connection with your dictum "I think, therefore, I am," there is a joke that occasionally surfaces even at present. I hope you will forgive me for repeating the joke now. In this joke, you go to a McDonald's to order a hamburger. When the clerk asks you whether you want mustard, you reply, "I don't think (so)"—whereupon you vanish from existence!

RD: Ha ha! Quel wit. Actually, I had myself raised this kind of possibility in my second "Meditation." (Of course, I did that simply on a premise that I would cease to think in general, not specifically about mustard on a hamburger.) My immediate answer to this contingency, as written in the Meditation, was that I would not cease to exist, because if I were thinking about not thinking, then I would have to exist to do that.

Of course, the joke depends on a semantic play on the word "think." You should adhere to my broader meaning of that word; to think is to be *immediately conscious of anything*.

BL: Because you put it that way, I would like to ask your opinion of how I deal with the concept of conscious experience. In my view, the essence of conscious experience is being *aware* of something. The *content* of an awareness can be anything. But being aware is a unique phenomenon in itself, independent of the nature of the particular content in awareness. Also, there is much evidence that what we may call thinking, as in the intuitive solutions to mathematical problems, can proceed unconsciously. That kind of thinking would then not constitute evidence for being consciously sure of one's existence.

RD: I think I could accept your view of conscious experience as being grounded in awareness. In a way it is closer to my view of the unassailable truth—that being aware is what I am really sure of and what proves I exist, whatever it is that I am aware of.

BL: I like your insistence that we should reject knowledge grounded in authority and that we must look for evidence to establish a truth. You further state that there is more than one way to deduce a cause for an effect, and that only an experiment can decide which alternative is valid. This view is remarkably close to modern experimental science, in which different hypotheses for explaining an observation are subject to experimental tests that can help to indicate which hypothesis is the superior one. Would you accept an application of this scientific method to test the validity of some of your proposals?

RD: Well, I would have to say yes, except for axiomatic principles that are untestable. The primary example of that is, of course, "cogito ergo sum." I know this intuitively as something that is irrefutable, although we may change that to "I am aware, therefore I am."

BL: I accept your qualification. I should add the qualification fostered by the philosopher of science, Karl Popper. Popper insisted that it must be possible to devise an experimental test that could potentially falsify or contradict a given proposed hypothesis. Otherwise, one could pro-pose any explanation without fear of its being contra-dicted. Such explanations would clearly not offer any definitive truths.

RD: I like Popper's way of making the evidence convincing. Well, what would you like to subject to such a scientific approach?

BL: Well, there is your proposal that the pineal gland is the focal site in the brain where the interaction between brain activities and the mind is arranged. Would you please tell us how you arrived at that proposal?

RD: Yes. I realized that thought is not divisible. For example, the conscious, subjective visual image is a unified or uni-tary "picture." That is, the conscious image is unified even though the messages from the eyes arrive at the brain via many individual nerve fibers in the optic nerves. Also, virtually all the structures in the brain are double, one on the left side matched by one on the right side. But the conscious sensory image is not double. In my view of the mechanical operations of the nervous system, I thought there must be a structure in the brain where the multitude of brain messages could be brought to a single focus for interaction with the mind, and not in a doubled fashion. Because the pineal gland was the only structure in the brain that was not doubled, it was a good candidate for the single focal site of interaction.

BL: The logic of your proposal is good. But it is not the only possible explanation for dealing with the unitary nature of thought or conscious experience. Indeed, some other proposals have recently appeared. Also, we know that the pineal gland receives only a tiny fraction of the brain's nerve pathways. So we should have further evidence to support the view that the pineal gland is really the focus of brain-mind interactions.

RD: Well, in my day, I must confess, we did not systematically search for evidence that uniquely supported an explanatory hypothesis, even though I had myself argued for that approach in principle. What would you suggest?

BL: An obvious test would be to see what happens if the pineal gland became nonfunctional. In such a case, your proposal would predict the loss of virtually all mind-brain interactions. Although your general dictum, cogito ergo sum, would mean that the person could still think and be conscious, the person would lose all awareness of and become nonresponsive at least to sensory messages in the brain. He would also lose the brain messages that lead the mind to perceive hunger, thirst, bodily pleasures, and so on. Furthermore, the mind/soul could no longer affect brain activity, so bodily acts in response to conscious will could not take place. The person would become paralyzed.

I must admit that it would not be easy or even ethical to deliberately destroy or inactivate the pineal gland in a living person. But one could at least look for possible cases of diseased pineal glands in autopsies of dead people and relate any such diseased condition to the behavior of the individual before death.

RD: I agree that a search for cases of diseased pineal glands at autopsies would be desirable and would be of interest as a test of the role of the pineal gland. I may note, however, that even you modern neuroscientists have not been able to establish a mechanism for mental unity with an experimental test.

BL: That is true. You proposed that the mind/soul and the

"body" (really all of the material world other than mind) are two separate substances—the res cogitans and res extensa, respectively. For you, the mind/soul substance could exist even if there were no body substance; indeed you noted that the existence of your thinking mind is the one thing you have no doubt of, whereas one cannot be as certain about the body's existence.

On the other hand, in a later writing, you state that the mind has its principal seat in the brain and that the soul does not perceive excepting insofar it is in the brain. And you note that the human mind is shown to be really distinct from the body, and nevertheless, to be so closely conjoined therewith, as together to form, as it were, a unity. That view is surprisingly similar to modern views. However, that view seems to blur the separation between mind and body. Could you clarify your position on this?

RD:  Mais oui. You have indeed raised a difficult point. However, I believe those statements of mine are not in conflict with my basic position. My acceptance of the brain as the structure that mediates the interaction between mind and body does not necessarily eliminate the view that the two are separate entities. How the two separate entities, mind and brain, accomplish the two-way interaction between them is a difficult question for which I proposed an answer; I assume you will want to deal with that, too.

BL:  Yes, but let's stick with the question of separateness for the moment. Would you allow for the alternative possibility that mind and brain are not in fact separate entities, but are somehow reflections or "properties" of a single entity? For example, it has been proposed that the mind "emerges" as a phenomenon related to certain activities of the system that constitutes the brain. As you may know, there is now an immense amount of evidence that mental, conscious processes are related to and dependent on specific structures and functions of the brain.

RD: Well, I suppose I cannot logically exclude the alternative that you describe. However, I have noted that mind and body differ in at least two fundamental ways. Mind cannot be conceived as divisible, while body is clearly divisible. Second, mind is a thinking thing while the body is a thing that has "extension." That is, the location and dimensions of the body can be measured. Because mind and body do not have these fundamental attributes in common, I concluded that these two "natures" or "substances" are separated one from the other. As I stated in the appendix to *Principles of Philosophy,* "two substances are said to be really distinct when each of them can exist without the other" (see Descartes, 1644).

BL: Well, I must respectfully argue that you cannot really know that mind and body can each exist without the other. That uncertainty makes the view of their distinct separateness a questionable one. However, I shall not push this issue further at present. I would prefer that you retain your equanimity and your friendly willingness to cooperate in this dialogue.

RD: Monsieur, I am, as you say, more mellow now, and I have promised not to become angry about opposing views. I will repeat, in relation to your last argument, the distinctions between mind and body, the former being indivisible and without extension, the latter divisible and possessing extension. This is in addition to the principle that the only existence I can be certain of is my own thinking mind. This means that mind and body are phenomenologically distinct and each is not describable by the other. However, I did recognize that brain and mind closely interact; the brain is where the mind is informed and affected by perceptions and where, in turn, the mind can induce the brain to control bodily actions.

In view of the immense accumulation in recent centuries of evidence that the mind is dependent on the brain for its manifestation, I could consider giving up the insistence that the mind and body substances can each exist without the other. Nevertheless, that would not exclude my proposal that mind and brain are separate things or entities—in other words, my so-called dualism. I may note here that I specifically stated that I would not say that this dualism indicated that the mind or soul is immortal. I had no way of knowing that immortality is real. That view contributed to my troubles with the Church. However, I did point out that one can *believe* in immortality as a matter of faith.

BL: Good. I accept the logic of your argument. I would like to commend you for your prescience in suggesting that it is only in the brain that the mind becomes informed of the sensory world. In several places you made the point that even if the sensory nerve from a given area of skin is excited at any point along its path to the brain, the mind would still perceive the sensation as located in the place of origin in the skin. That is, every sensation is perceived only by an interaction at the brain, between the sensory message and the mind. But, subjectively, the sensation is perceived as coming from its normal point of origin in the skin regardless of the point in the sensory pathway at which the message was initiated. In modern terminology, I would say the sensation is subjectively referred to a proper point in space, even though the pattern of the corresponding activities in the brain may not look like the subjective image of it. I shall be discussing this phenomenon at some length elsewhere in relation to our experimental evidence.

RD: Well, it is gratifying indeed that my view of the way a sensation is transmitted to the mind, which I described 350 years ago, still makes sense today.

BL: There is another important issue on which I would like your comments. In your views about the mind, you appear to restrict its nature to the presence of conscious experience.

RD: Mais oui. I could only be certain of the existence of my conscious thinking. As we have already discussed, by thinking, I meant an immediate consciousness of something.

BL: Yes, a clearly defensible position. However, in more recent centuries, considerable evidence has appeared to indicate that many of our mental processes are conducted unconsciously, without awareness. Direct evidence has appeared in the last few decades (see Chapters 2 and 3). But long before that, we had much convincing clinical and anecdotal evidence. For example, the great French mathematician Poincaré described how the solution to a difficult problem suddenly appeared in his conscious mind, without his having been aware of the way in which the solution was achieved. That is, the whole complex creative process toward solution of the problem had proceeded unconsciously. Is it possible to fit such unconscious processes into your view of yourself as a "thinking thing"?

RD: I must admit that the evidence for unconscious mental operations is convincing. Nevertheless, if we turn back to my cogito ergo sum, it is clear that I can only be certain of the existence of my conscious thought. I cannot be certain of the existence of a mental process of which I am not aware.

On the other hand, having scientific evidence to distinguish between alternative hypotheses is the best route toward truth. And so I would be willing to say that the existence of unconscious mental processes seems most probably true, based on the evidence for it, although I cannot say that with the certainty I have about the existence of my conscious thinking.

BL: Well, on that note, let me cite some experimental evidence that directly confirms the existence of an unconscious mental process. Subjects received electrical stimuli to an ascending sensory pathway in the brain. With a sufficiently long lasting train of electrical pulses (up to 500 msec), they could report having a conscious sensation. With short trains of stimulus pulses (100 to 200 msec), the subjects could not consciously feel any sensations. But they could fairly accurately report that a stimulus had been delivered, even though they felt nothing! In an analogous kind of experiment (by Weiskrantz, 1986), patients who had lost conscious vision (because of a lesion in the primary visual receiving area of the cerebral cortex) could nevertheless correctly point to the location of an object that they could not consciously see (so-called blindsight).

RD: That does produce convincing evidence for the existence of unconscious mental processes, but I still think that conclusion does not achieve the certainty I have about the existence of my conscious thinking (or feeling, and so on).

BL: Let me ask about your view on the existence of free will.

RD: Oh, I think there is little doubt that we have free choice for at least some of our actions.

BL: You may be interested to hear about our experimental findings on this issue. We found that the brain begins to initiate and prepare for a voluntary act about 400 msec before the person becomes consciously aware of his or her intention or wish to act. That means that conscious free will does not initiate the volitional process; the brain initiates the process unconsciously.

RD: So is there any possibility for free will to have a role in volition?

BL: Yes. Conscious intention does appear about 150 msec before the motor act. That leaves sufficient time for the conscious function to intervene in the process. It may provide a trigger to enable the volitional process to go to completion; however, there is no direct evidence for that. But there is evidence that the conscious will can stop or veto the process so that no act occurs. In such a case, free will could control the outcome. That fits with our feeling that we can control ourselves, something that ethical systems urge us to do.

RD: I am glad to hear of that role for conscious will. Now, how do you relate all this to the argument by the determinists that we really are automatons, completely subject to the natural physical laws of the universe?

BL: That is a complicated question. But I think we can fall back to your own view on what to believe. That is, we can know with certainty what we ourselves are consciously aware of. We are aware of feeling that we can control the appearance of a voluntary act, including what to do or when to do it. That is a strong argument for actual free will. Determinism works well for the physical world, but it is only a theory when applied to the conscious mental sphere.

RD: Again, I am delighted that this fundamental aspect of my philosophy still has crucial merit.

BL: Well, M. Descartes, merci beaucoup for your participation and patience in this dialogue.

### How May Our Experimental Findings Affect How You View Yourself?

We now know something about what nerve cells have to be doing to support or mediate the appearance of a conscious subjective experience, in particular, awareness. These are unique neural activities that must be superimposed on the background functions of a relatively normal brain. The special neural activities center around time factors (see also Poppel, 1988).

Conscious mental events appear only after a minimum duration of activations. This is as long as 0.5 sec or more, though shorter than 0.5 sec with stronger activities. Unconscious mental events do not require such long-lasting activations. They can appear even with very brief neural activations, lasting as little as 0.1 sec or less. This describes my time-on theory, to provide a controlling factor in the transition between conscious and unconscious functions.

The time-on feature means that our conscious experience of our sensory world is delayed by a significant time. As the *Göteborg-Post*, the leading newspaper in Göteborg, Sweden, put it in their headline poster (when reporting on my lecture in May, 1993), "Now it has been proven: We are all somewhat behind." We are not consciously living in the actual present!

So, there is the unexpected evidence that there is a substantial delay, up to about 500 msec, in our conscious experience of the sensory world. Admittedly, this was thoroughly established only for bodily sensations, but indirect evidence makes it likely to be applicable to all sensory modalities.

But strangely, we are not aware of this delay. There is subjective antedating of the delayed experience, back to the time of the fastest response of the sensory cerebral cortex. We called this "subjective referral backwards in time." This allows us to feel that we are aware of a sensory signal almost immediately, when in fact the awareness could not have appeared before the delay required by the duration of appropriate neural activity for developing the awareness.

On the other hand, the delay in the actual appearance of awareness makes sense for other mental phenomena.

*Unconscious* mental events do not require such long-lasting neural activations. As stated above, they can appear even with very brief delays lasting 100 msec or less. (Our experimental evidence for my time-on theory provided direct proof for this.) Fast responses to sensory signals are developed unconsciously. These are evident in almost all sports activities, but also in everyday responses to danger signals. There is experimental evidence that responses in tests for reaction times (RTs) are made unconsciously. The *origin* of words being spoken in a normal stream must be unconscious in nature as is the playing of musical instruments, especially for fast runs of notes.

Of course, in all these cases, you can become *aware* of the response or action after it has occurred. If you try to become aware of the action before making it, the whole process is slowed and becomes much less effective.

We may extrapolate the delay feature to all instances of awareness. That would mean that all mental events with awareness would be preceded by unconscious processes that begin up to 500 msec before awareness. Note that there is no antedating process available to subjectively affect most awarenesses. Antedating can occur only for conscious sensations responding to sensory signals. Therefore, all of our conscious thoughts would be initiated unconsciously and be delayed by up to 500 msec following their unconscious beginnings. In other words, all of our conscious thoughts would arise unconsciously! That would be true even for creative and complex mental operations. Surely, that must put a fundamental qualification on our view of how all such thinking arises. It also suggests that we should nurture the conditions in which free play of unconscious mental activity may proceed.

There could not be a continuous stream of consciousness if there were a substantial delay in the production of a conscious event. Conscious events would have to appear discontinuously. The fact that we ordinarily experience being conscious in a continuous manner can be explained by an overlap in the appearance of multiple conscious events.

The modification or distortion of a subjective experience is a well-accepted phenomenon in psychiatry and psychology. Freud proposed that emotionally charged sensory images and thoughts could be repressed unconsciously. A subject who was upset by having seen a mangled dead body may report having seen a distortion of that image or even no image at all.

To modify a sensory image, there would have to be time available after the sensory messages arrived at the cerebral cortex. During such a delay, the brain could react to the image and generate neural patterns to modify it before the subject became consciously aware of the image. The physiological requirement of a delay for development of awareness provides an opportunity for unconscious cerebral processes to modify the content of a subjective experience. Indeed, we showed that stimulation of sensory cortex, applied hundreds of msec after a stimulus to the skin, could retroactively either depress or enhance the subject's experience of that skin stimulus.

Finally, there is the discovery that the brain unconsciously initiates the volitional process well before a person becomes aware of an intention or wish to act voluntarily. That result clearly has a profound impact on how we view the nature of free will and on issues of personal responsibility and guilt (see Chapter 5).

The various examples described here show how the time factor for awareness can have a profound impact on our conscious mental life.

At this point, the comments of philosopher David M. Rosenthal (2002) are appropriate. These appeared in the June 2002 issue of *Consciousness and Cognition,* a special issue devoted to timing relations between brain and world that was primarily devoted to commentaries on my work in this area. (There are a number of other critical and supportive commentaries on our work in this issue. I have now had the opportunity to write and publish my replies to most of them; see Libet, 2003)

Rosenthal states that he has "little to say in this brief note about Libet's experimental work." He argues that there is an "apparent conflict of Libet's results with common sense," and so this "adds to the reasons we already have to reject the picture on which that conflict seems to arise." The "picture" Rosenthal has in mind refers to our experimental evidence for delays in achieving awareness, in the case of conscious sensation, and in the appearance of the conscious wish or urge to act (relative to the prior unconscious initiation of the volitional process by the brain).

Rosenthal's chief argument is that the general commonsense picture of such events is in conflict with our experimental findings. He believes that makes our experimental conclusions unlikely to be valid. He does note that a person's ability to veto the performance of a volitional urge to act "might mitigate the conflict somewhat, but only if we have independent evidence that this conscious veto does not itself occur after a nonconscious neural veto." I have analyzed this latter issue at some length (Libet, 1999), and showed that the evidence is compatible with the view that the conscious veto arises without the preparatory nonconscious processes having made the final decision to veto.

Rosenthal goes on to argue that "our commonsense picture plainly accommodates nonconscious volitions." But that argument seems to defeat his point regarding the commonsense paradox, which is that our findings "compromise our sense of free agency." He then claims that our findings of unconscious initiation of the volitional process are actually quite compatible with our commonsense picture! If you want to accept unconscious initiations of voluntary acts as not in conflict with your feelings of free agency, you can certainly do so. But then you would have trouble with the concepts of responsibility and guilt for the initiations over which you have no conscious control. Conscious control only comes with the potential for veto of the process before the final act occurs.

Rosenthal seems to share the approach to our productions that many philosophers share: Untested philosophical models and speculative views may be proposed as if they were capable of contradicting conclusions that are based on experimental evidence. As scientists, we cannot accept that. Proposed models or theories are valuable only if they help explain the data, not when they contradict the data. A "commonsense" view cannot supercede hard-gained experimental data. Experimental discoveries often present counterintuitive results and inferences that are original and creative. There is perhaps nothing more counterintuitive and in conflict with commonsense than quantum theory. Yet it is regarded as a major pillar of physics and correctly predicts experimental observations.

## How Should We View Self and Soul?

We come finally to consider the nature of the self and the soul in relation to conscious functions of the brain. Are they special cases of conscious processes, or are they in separate categories that are independent of conscious processes generally? Do they emerge from appropriate activities of nerve cells in the brain? Or are they entities that are separate from the physical brain, in a Cartesian sense? On this last point, we must recognize that there is no evidence to support the concept of separate entity status, which can only be a metaphysical belief. I therefore base further discussion on the view that the self and the soul are emergent phenomena of brain activity.

Certainly, these phenomena can be altered or abolished by pharmacological agents and by pathological changes of the brain. Think, for example, of the loss of selfhood in Alzheimer's disease, associated with structural and biochemical changes in the brain.

There have been many views expressed regarding the nature, origins, and meanings of self (von Weiszaker noted that "[it] is characteristic of psychology not to really ask what soul is"; quoted in Del Guidice, 1993). Most of these represent philosophical analyses and interesting speculations. I would like to limit the discussion here to the simplest phenomenal features of self—in other words, to those features that are reportable experiences by most human beings. A primary status for such reportable phenomena is adopted as the basis of the book by Karl Popper and John C. Eccles (1977), *The Self and Its Brain,* a title that is a reversal of the more common view of a brain and *its* self.

The simplest phenomenological view of self is the subjective feeling we each have of being our own person, with a unique personal identity. Neurologist Antonio Damasio (1999) proposes a distinction between a transient self (that is continuously generated as a result of one's ongoing experiences of the sensory world), and an autobiographical self (based on memories of experiences and so on). Damasio refers to the former, transient self as a "core self." I prefer to reserve the term "core self" for an enduring aspect of self, the personal identity one feels even when there are significant and even extreme changes in the content of one's capacities for conscious experience.

The resistance to change, for what I am calling the core self, is quite remarkable. Even after temporary loss of consciousness due to a variety of causes, people know who they are upon returning to consciousness. The same phenomenon occurs after a person awakes from ordinary sleep, general anesthesia, or even a long coma. Lesions of the cerebral cortex can be quite extensive without loss of personal identity, although many mental and conscious functions may be distorted or abolished.

In split-brain patients (in whom the main neural connections between the two cerebral hemispheres have been cut), each hemisphere can possess knowledge of events not available to the other hemisphere. Yet these people show no evidence of difficulties with their personal identities. They do not complain of having multiple personalities; they still feel they are the single individual they were before the splitting of the interconnections.

The same is true even in patients in whom a whole cerebral hemisphere has been excised or destroyed by pathological conditions such as a large tumor. Their awareness of personal identity is continuous in spite of drastic losses in mental functions such as paralysis and loss of sensation on one side or a speech loss if the dominant (usually the left) hemisphere is gone. I have viewed a video of such a patient who seemed convincingly aware of, and responsive to, an interviewer. Yet he knew all too well what his deficiencies were.

Further, patients with bilateral lesions in the hippocampal structures in their temporal lobes lose the ability to form new explicit memories, but they retain memories of events that occurred before the injury. These patients also appear to know who they are and are even aware of their loss of memory formation.

Even complete amnesia concerning past history or even one's name does not appear to destroy the sense of self. Of course, there is no autobiographical self *during* the amnesia, yet it can reappear when the patient recovers from the amnesia. In a recently reported case, a young woman suffered complete amnesia after being struck into a coma by an automobile, but she did recover full consciousness. After two years in amnesia, this patient began to recall and express past events, beginning with her suddenly shouting "Joyce," which was part of her real name. (She had been called Jane Doe by attendants.) After she was able to recall her Social Security number, she was identified. Next came a rapid restoration of memories concerning her past. Her feeling of personal identity was not permanently destroyed by the loss of her autobiographical self for two years!

### How Does Self Relate to Awareness?

I proposed in an earlier chapter that awareness is a fundamental phenomenon, with its own unique requirements of neural activities. I also proposed that the different contents in awareness may account for the variety of conscious experiences, without our having to regard the different classes of experiences as different kinds of awareness. I include the phenomenon of self in that view. That is, the experience of selfhood may represent a kind of content added to awareness. Theorists have produced a variety of selves to account for the actual variety in phenomenological displays of a self. It is simpler to view these varieties of self as variations in the *contents* of basic awareness rather than as different levels and kinds of awarenesses.

There is a puzzling question in this view of the primacy of awareness. When there is awareness of some mental "contents," whether these contents include the feeling of self or simply sensory stimuli, who is aware of that mental content? The idea that there is a personal entity that experiences these contents is not popular with most philosophers and neuroscientists. Any such personal entity cannot be viewed as a specific neural configuration in some localized part of the brain. Large lesions in any part of the cerebral hemispheres do not abolish awareness and personal identity, though it is true that a lesion in the medial intralaminar nucleus of thalamus or in the reticular formation in the brain stem can abolish conscious awareness completely. That has led some to propose such an area as the locus for consciousness. But these structures are best regarded as necessary for keeping the cerebral cortex awake, rather than as centers sufficient for the whole experience. We are forced to think of a more global representation of consciousness and the self that is produced by whatever brain areas remain sufficient after large lesions.

I come back to my proposed conscious mental field (CMF), to which almost any part of the cortex may contribute, as a potential answer to our question: A unified experience of awareness is the postulated attribute of the CMF. See Chapter 5 for a description of CMF and an experimental design to test that theory. The CMF would provide the kind of global attributes needed for subjective unity and for the "who" that is aware of mental contents.

### Are Unconscious Mental Processes Part of Self?

Much of our mental life proceeds unconsciously, and unconscious mental processes can affect succeeding conscious processes. Some of the simplest examples of this principle lie in the findings of Shevrin (1973), using very brief visual stimuli (about 1 msec) whose contents were not consciously discerned by the subjects. Shevrin and Dickman (1980) showed that the contents of these unconscious inputs distinctly affected the subjects' selection of word responses from a list of new words. That is, the selected new words showed an association with the items "observed" unconsciously. So these unconscious perceptions had an impact on later mental operations. Analogous results were found with patients after recovery from general anesthesia

(Bennett et al, 1985; Bonke et al., 1986). Vocal expressions in the operating room were not consciously heard and could not be recalled later, but they still had an impact on the patients' responses after recovery.

Unconscious mental processes are in fact unique for a given individual. For example, a mathematician may solve a problem unconsciously, something that someone else does not do. It may seem appropriate, then, to regard one's unconscious mental life as belonging to, and characteristic of, one's self. However, one does not have direct experiential access to the unconscious mental processes, although these processes may have an impact on how we view ourselves consciously. Chapter 4 considered the question of responsibility and guilt for unconscious volitional processes. In my view, the crucial point is that we have *conscious control* over the actual performance of our unconsciously initiated volitional process. Hence, we are responsible for our conscious control choices, not for our unconsciously initiated urges that precede our conscious decisions.

### Is the Feeling of Self a Singular Experience?

The most direct challenge to the singular uniqueness of a personal self comes from the alleged existence of multiple personality disorder (MPD). In MPD, a patient appears to exhibit more than one personality at different times. There seems to be one personality that prevails most of the time, and it remains as the sole personality when therapy successfully eliminates the others. The various personalities can be strikingly different and exhibit behaviors virtually opposite to those of the main personality. Some readers may remember the old movie *The Three Faces of Eve,* adapted from a nonfiction book of that title by Hervey Cleckley. There was, of course, Stevenson's *Dr. Jekyll and Mr.*

*Hyde,* published in 1886, but this was a fictional tale with no relation to clinical evidence.

A science writer named Flora R. Schreiber (1973) published *Sybil* based on clinical reports by Sybil's psychiatrist Cornelia Wilbur. The case appeared to be a documented example of MPD, and thus helped to establish a diagnosis of MPD as a genuine disorder in psychiatric practice.

However, the validity of the Sybil story and diagnosis was seriously questioned by Herbert Spiegel (1997), a psychiatrist and expert in hypnosis. Spiegel had considerable direct contact with Sybil for several years, as an adjunct to the therapy by Wilbur. In a lengthy published interview (*The New York Review of Books,* April 24, 1997), Spiegel called Sybil's diagnosis of MPD into question. He discovered that Sybil was highly hypnotizable. During an age-regression under hypnosis, Sybil reported the usual events of a child, but not the stories of parental abuse that Wilbur got. In one such session, Sybil asked Spiegel if he wanted her to be Helen, a name that Wilbur had given her for a feeling she had. Indeed, Sybil felt an obligation to become another personality; but with Spiegel, she preferred *not* to "be Helen." There were many further indications to support Spiegel's view that the MPD phenomenon of Sybil was an artifact that was created by Wilbur. Spiegel realized that Wilbur was not sufficiently knowledgeable about hypnotic manifestations and that Wilbur had been reifying a memory of some kind and converting it into a personality. Spiegel suggested that any highly hypnotizable patient who has been diagnosed as MPD is almost certainly not a real case of MPD. Other MPDs who are not highly hypnotizable can also be misdiagnosed for other reasons.

On the other hand, Spiegel does note there are "people with transient disassociations (in their views of self), where they temporarily lose their sense of identity." He then "puts them together" right away, "to restore a sense of control as soon as possible."

We see, then, that the challenge to the single-self view from the reports of MPD is, at best, a doubtful one. However, temporary loss of personal identity can apparently occur. But with recovery from that loss the person again feels she is the same person as before.

### Does a Split Brain Affect Personhood?

In a split-brain patient, the commissures, which are the bundles of nerve fibers that connect the two cerebral hemispheres, have been surgically cut through to relieve certain types of epilepsy. "[M]ost of the conscious experience generated within one hemisphere becomes inaccessible to the conscious awareness of the other" (Sperry, 1985). A series of studies by Sperry et al. (1969) showed that "these people live with two largely separate left and right domains of inner consciousness. Each hemisphere can be shown to experience its own private sensations, percepts, thoughts, and memories, which are inaccessible to awareness in the other hemisphere." All the tests indicated that the right hemisphere is conscious and, except for lacking an ability to speak, it exhibits thoughtful, logical, and emotional activities, separate from but equal in quality to those of the left hemisphere (see also Bogen, 1986; Doty, 1999). (There have been disagreements with this view; see Gazzaniga, 1998.)

All this evidence indicates that it is possible for the single self to be two in nature. Yet the split-brain patients appear to be single-minded, unified individuals. They do not complain of any loss of personal identity or of split experiences. Sperry (1985) offers some explanations for this situation. Awareness involving self and social factors generated in one hemisphere could promptly spread to the other. This could be mediated by deep interconnecting structures that are not divided by the upper commissurotomies. Also, there are bilateral representations for the face, for audition, and for other systems that are not dependent on the upper commissures. Division of the visual fields can be made ineffective by having both eyes roaming over the entire visual field.

So it would seem that, although some aspects of the conscious self can be split in these patients, the conscious self is largely unified. That unified self is especially predominant in normal people.

### Do Identical Twins Have One or Two Separate Selves?

Identical twins stem from a single fertilized egg and have identical genetic makeup in all their cells. However, the *expression* of genes is dependent on the conditions of brain development and the effects of environment through life. Identity of genes, therefore, does not necessarily mean identity of the actual individuals. Nevertheless, identical twins who have been separated and reared in different environments exhibit remarkable similarities in mental outlook, choices of mates, autos, behaviors, as well as their physical appearances. But identical twins feel they are unique persons. Each knows who she is and does not confuse herself with the other twin. Identical twins do not, therefore, provide an example of a split self.

When, then does a unique self appear? Some religious systems hold that a self or soul is "attached" to the fertilized egg at conception. But identical twins start out as a single fertilized egg, yet they develop into two independent selves. It would seem more likely that some form of a self appears when the fetus has a brain of sufficient structure and form to support conscious experience.

### Do Computers Have a Conscious Self?

Some computer enthusiasts, especially those working in artificial intelligence, have expressed a belief that computers may be conscious. They feel that if and when a computer is as complex as the human brain, and can behave in a way not distinguishable from that of a person, the computer should be regarded as functionally equivalent to a human person. In the famous Turing paradigm, this would happen when a computer behind a screen could give responses indistinguishable from those of a person behind the screen (of course, there is no guarantee that this would happen).

There have been a number of physical and philosophical arguments made in opposition to such a view. The mathematical physicist Roger Penrose (1989) has argued that computers are always operating with a programmed algorithm. But, he notes, conscious mental functions can be nonalgorithmic and are thus fundamentally different from computer functions. Penrose "demonstrates that neither quantum theory nor classical physics shed any light on the question of determinism vs. free will." He states that "our present science is incomplete" (see review by Palm, 1991). Philosopher John Searle (1980) points out that a computer can respond to questions based on its programming for the syntax of the language. It can thus appear to respond like a human person. But, unlike the person, the computer does not understand the meaning of the language. The computer can be programmed for syntax, but not for the semantics of the language. This distinction between syntax and semantics, as an important issue for consciousness, was expressed earlier (in 1953) by the philosopher Karl Popper.

I have pointed out (Libet, 1980) that even if there were identical behavioral functions for a computer and a person, as in the Turing paradigm, that cannot necessarily be taken to mean that the computer is therefore also conscious, like a person. The proof of this statement lies in a simple logical argument. One is dealing here with two different systems: A (the computer) and B (the person). A and B are known to be different in many ways—for example, in the materials of which they are constructed. The two different systems, A and B, are found to give identical behavioral responses to questions (if the Turing paradigm ever does work). Does that mean that the two systems are also identical in other characteristics, like the possession of consciousness? The answer to that is no, based on simple rules of logic. That is, if system A exhibits X and system B exhibits X, it does not follow that both systems will exhibit Y (even if one of them does exhibit Y). Systems that are similar in one respect need not be similar in other properties.

Such a logical fallacy also applies to another related contention. It has been suggested that we might replace each nerve cell in the brain with a silicon chip that performs all of the same functions. If we could do this for the whole brain, we might have an instrument that could perform functions indistinguishable from those of the original brain. This zombie, according to some, would also be conscious. But, again, this is a different system from the original brain and it cannot be said to share all the properties of the normal brain. The brain is structurally and functionally different from a system of silicon chips.

### What Is Meant by the Soul?

It is not easy to distinguish the meaning of soul from that of self. For many people, soul appears to refer to a more spiritual meaning and feeling than does self. There is also a tendency to feel that the soul has a deeper inner meaning than self. Many religious systems consider the soul as an inner substance that can leave the body after death and live on forever. This view is, at present, a metaphysical belief: It cannot be falsified by any evidence.

Just as the phenomenon of self may be a special case of a kind of content in basic awareness, so may a phenomenon of soul be such a case, if indeed there are real differences between self and soul.

Neither self nor soul need be physical substances although they emerge from physical activities of nerve cells. The phenomenological feeling of their existence may be based on special kinds of neural processes. Feelings of self and soul can be destroyed by extensive neural damage, as in advanced Alzheimer's disease or in Creutzfeldt-Jacob disease. This may occur even when awareness has not been completely eliminated. So, feelings of self and soul do require a sufficiently structured and functional brain.

Soulful feelings have strong meanings for many people and should be taken to be serious phenomena based on appropriate neuronal activities. Soulful feelings are especially important to, and expressed in, music, art, literature, and, of course, religious and spiritual activities. Such phenomenal feelings should not be dismissed lightly, without convincing counterevidence.

As an example of this view of the soul, I quote from the writings of the eminent novelist Saul Bellow. Bellow cannot be accused of basing his views on a religious indoctrination, as he is a very secular person. The following quotes are from a review by Leon Wieseltier (1987). Writing of his novel *Herzog*, Bellow (1987) notes that "a Ph.D. from a good American university [Herzog] falls apart when his wife leaves him for another man. What is he to do in this moment of crisis, pull Aristotle or

Spinoza from the shelf and storm through the pages looking for consolation and advice?" Looking back on Herzog, Bellow notes that "in the greatest confusion there is still an open channel to the soul. It may be difficult to find because by midlife it is over-grown, and some of the wildest thickets surrounding it grow out of what we describe as our education. But the channel is al-ways there, and it is our business to keep it open, to have access to the deepest part of ourselves—to that part of us which is con-scious of a higher consciousness, by means of which we make final judgments and put everything together. The independence of this consciousness, which has the strength to be immune to the noise of history and the distractions of our immediate sur-roundings, is what the life struggle is all about. The soul has to find and hold its ground against hostile forces, sometimes em-bodied in ideas which frequently deny its very existence, and which indeed often seem to be trying to annul it altogether." Wieseltier comments, "These wise and beautiful sentences cap-ture the objective of Bellow's book perfectly." And "Bellow has discerned the far-reaching difference between intellectual life and contemplative life. And also that there are significant ele-ments of a modern intellectual's education that must be un-learned if a beginning is to be made." Obviously, Bellow's views are opposed to those of many theorists, especially materialist determinists.

There have been many other expressions against the material-ist determinist doctrine that any feelings of self, soul, and free will are illusions; that we are automatons governed by the inexo-rable adherence to established physical laws; and that a knowl-edge of the structures and functions of the elements in the brain will tell us everything about conscious experience and its mani-festations. The latter view is known as reductionism.

The issues of determinism, reductionism, and free will have

been discussed in Chapters 4 and 5. I can say categorically that there is nothing in neuroscience or in modern physics that compels us to accept the theories of determinism and reductionism. In addition to my arguments in Chapters 4 and 5, there are those of Sperry (1985), Popper and Eccles (1977), and of many physicists.

The University of Cambridge physicist Sir Brian Pippard (1992) notes that if a theory of everything "meant only the material world it would not be so bad, but it also includes the human mind." But "the very ground rules of science,—preclude its finding an explanation for my consciousness, the one phenomenon of which I am absolutely certain." I would qualify this by referring to our own experimental research on conscious experience; in these scientifically conducted studies, reports of conscious experience were accepted as valid information about the actual subjective experiences (see Chapters 1 and 2).

The physicist Brian D. Josephson (1993) wrote a report on a symposium dealing with reductionism in science and culture. He reported that physicists, mathematicians, and philosophers in that symposium considered reductionism to be unacceptable and misleading.

In any case, the phenomena of self or soul, and the potentially causative role they may have in mind-brain interactions, are not made meaningless by any determinist, materialist, or reductionist theory.

### Is There Life after Death?

Some semblance of evidence for life after death has come from the reports of persons who have had near-death experiences. People who experience cardiac arrest go through stages of loss of cerebral functions. There is an initial phase in which various functions are lost. Even after all functions are gone, there is a longer time period (of about 5 minutes) during which it is possible to restore cerebral functions if circulation of blood to the brain is resumed during that time. That is, the damage that is occurring during this time is potentially reversible. With longer periods of cardiac arrest, damage becomes progressively irreversible.

Cardiac arrest may appear suddenly, as when the major pumping heart muscle (the ventricles) suddenly becomes disorganized (fibrillation) and ineffective as a pump of the blood. The stoppage of circulation of blood to the brain results in a progressive loss of function for different parts of the brain. The cerebral (and cerebellar) cortex ceases activity within 5 to 10 sec, so that consciousness and then the electrical rhythms (brain waves or electroencephalogram) disappear in that time. The subcortical parts of the brain are a bit more resistant; but after about 30 sec, even the lower brain stem goes out, with a loss of breathing and other bodily controls that have their centers in the medulla. The spinal cord, and the simple reflexes it mediates, survives a bit longer (for 1 to 2 min).

When all these brain activities are lost, the person seems, for all intents and purposes, to be dead. However, if the heart can be induced to resume effective pumping within a maximum period of about 5 min, the various functions of the brain can recover, though it may take weeks for full recovery. During the 5-min period of arrest, metabolic degradation of nerve cells goes on because of the absence of oxygen and glucose, which provides cellular energy, and the accumulation of metabolites in and around neurons. The other organs of the body, including the heart, can withstand much longer periods of circulatory arrest before the effects become irreversible. It is thus possible to restart the heart after the 5-min deadline for brain revivability. When the heart is restarted after 5 min, the body can be maintained in a living state with artificial respiration but with a dead brain. When the brain is irreversibly dead, an individual can never recover from a coma.

Persons who have recovered from cardiac arrest have reported having had experiences during the time the brain was functionally inactive or "dead." A common report is of floating about in the operating room and watching the doctors and nurses attempting resuscitation. Another one is of the patient feeling that he is proceeding into a tunnel with a bright light at the end. These reports may include a feeling of peacefulness associated with the tunnel and light.

What can we make of such reports? If the brain were completely inactive ("dead") when these reported experiences occurred, we might have some impressively convincing evidence of extracorporeal psychic existence. But there are some difficulties with these data. First, it is astonishing that a person could remember such subjective experiences for later reporting. Presumably, the brain structures that mediate formation of a memory were also inoperative during the cardiac arrest. Second, persons who report floating about and observing the resuscitation process could be reporting recollections of scenes, observed or imagined, that were formed before the cardiac arrest. Third, we may question how thoroughly the condition of complete absence of brain functions was established in persons giving the reported experiences. For example, in some early work, I (along with my colleagues) established that a clap of hands produced an initial "primary evoked electrical response" at the auditory cortex. This response appeared for a time after the spontaneous electrical rhythms associated with consciousness disappeared.

(The subject was a cat, but there is reason to believe that a similar result would appear in a human subject.)

An experiment that could produce a rigorously convincing answer to this profoundly important issue of an afterlife is very difficult to achieve. If a subject with a cardiac pacemaker could be available for a special experiment with cardiac arrest for 3–4 min, a rigorous test situation could be arranged. (This could not be done using a patient in the emergency room with spontaneous cardiac arrest.) The test would involve turning off the pacemaker to produce a cardiac arrest lasting 3 to 4 min, well within the limits for recovery of brain function. Before the patient was brought into the room, unusual and strange images and sounds would be introduced but covered up in the room. These would be exposed after the loss of brain functions in the cardiac arrest. When active resuscitation to restore cardiac beating and pumping of blood was begun, the medical personnel would immediately remove the special gowns and images and the veils for the wall pictures would be reapplied.

When the patient was again conscious and responsive, she could be asked to report any experiences that happened during the procedure. If the patient reported having floated about the room and observing the medical personnel, she could be asked to describe the backs of those personnel and anything observed about the room's walls and so forth. If the patient correctly reported seeing the secreted indicators, that would be remarkably convincing for the validity of the report. However, if the patient reported seeing the usual environment of the room instead of the secreted one, the report's validity would collapse. Some other explanation of what is reported in the "after death" situation would have to be sought.

Of course, the difficulty with this experiment is that the team would have to act within the time periods of cardiac arrest. In addition, it is not likely that the experiment would be approved by an institution's committee for the protection of human patients.

Another workable design for testing whether the dead can communicate with the living has been activated by two scientists at the University of Arizona (Schwartz and Russek), whose work was described by Ann Japenga (1999). This design allows normal individuals to participate. Each participant stores a message known only to him in a computer. The computer scrambles the message into code. After death, the participant communicates by telepathy with an arranged person who is still alive. The phrase that unlocks the code is presumably given by the dead person to the living colleague.

Actually, this kind of experiment has, I believe, been conducted and failed. In the early 1900s, the great magician Houdini arranged for a similar kind of test of whether he would be able to communicate with a living person after his own death. Houdini died not long thereafter, but his widow and friends reported that they did not receive any messages from him.

There have of course been claims by some who call themselves mediums that they can call up a speaking ghost of a dead individual, but these demonstrations in séances have routinely been exposed as fraudulent when investigated by an expert.

I have no objection to the possibility of some kind of meaningful existence of a soul after death. In fact, such a condition could make the prospect of death profoundly more palatable. However, we still have not gone beyond metaphysical beliefs on this issue. As we have seen, the question is extremely difficult to answer in any scientifically convincing manner.

For the present, then, we may accept the concept of a "soul" as based on phenomenologically meaningful experiences. These experiences do not prove there is an actual entity, the soul, but neither is such a possibility disproven. The attack by the philosopher Gilbert Ryle on the Cartesian concept of a separable soul called that proposed entity "the ghost in the machine." But Ryle's attack is based on his belief that we are just machines. How does Ryle *know* there is no ghost in our cerebral makeup? The fact is he does not know. There is no direct evidence that contradicts the possible existence of a Cartesian-type soul. But there is also no evidence that contradicts a nonphysical phenomenon that is not separable from the brain (as in my CMF theory). Nor is there evidence that confirms it, as yet.

### In Conclusion

Let me repeat what I said at the beginning: Our subjective inner life is what really matters to us as human beings. Yet we know and understand relatively little of how it arises and how it functions in our conscious will to act. We do know that, in the only life we know, the physical brain is essential to and intimately involved in the manifestation of our conscious subjective experience.

In this book, I have introduced some of the experimental progress toward discovering the significant physical neuronal activities that mediate nonphysical conscious subjective experiences. I emphasized our research, partly to give you a glimpse into how such discoveries are made and also to provide a basis for the conclusions and inferences I made from the evidence. Also, our research provides rare findings into the relationship between neural activities and subjective experience, findings based on direct intracranial studies of neural stimulations and recordings. It has allowed us to establish the causal nature of relationships, not merely the correlations.

We discovered that a time factor appears to be a significant element in the way awareness is produced and in the transition between unconscious mental functions and conscious ones.

Even these limited discoveries that center on the time factor would appear to have a profound effect on how we view our mental selves. If all conscious awarenesses are preceded by unconscious processes, we are forced to conclude that we do not actually live in the present and that unconscious processes play a predominant role in the production of our conscious life. We found that this can be extended even to an unconscious initiation of a voluntary act and appears to restrict the role of free will to controlling the performance of actions. We have also seen that subjective experiences of all kinds involve a subjective referral of the responsible brain activities into images or thoughts that give a conscious order and meaning to the complicated neural activities that elicit them.

Our surprising discoveries could not have been made without the intracranial access we had to certain parts of the brain in collaborative human subjects.

My chief concluding hopes are: (1) that you have absorbed our experimental discoveries on the mind-brain problem; (2) that you recognize how those discoveries may affect your views about your own mental experiences; and finally (3) that a qualified experimental neurosurgery group will carry out an appropriate test of my unified cerebral mental field theory (see Chapter 5). I have already provided an experimental design for such a test. The result of the proposed test could falsify and disprove the theory. But a positive result, one showing subjective communication and intentional actions without any neural connections, would have a profound impact on how we view the nature of conscious experience and on neuroscience generally.

BIBLIOGRAPHY

INDEX

# BIBLIOGRAPHY

Amassian, V. E., M. Somasunderinn, J. C. Rothswell, J. B. Crocco, P. J. Macabee, and B. L. Day. 1991. Parasthesias are elicited by single pulse magnetic coil stimulation of motorcortex in susceptible humans. *Brain* 114:2505–2520.

Baars, B. J. 1988. *A Cognitive Theory of Consciousness*. Cambridge, England: Cambridge University Press.

Barbur, J. L., J. D. G. Watson, R. S. J. Frackowiak, and S. Zeki. 1993. Conscious visual perception without VI. *Brain* 116:1293–1302.

Bellow, S. 1987. *More Die of Heartbreak*. New York: Morrow.

Bennett, H. L., H. S. Davis, and J. A. Giannini. 1985. Nonverbal response to intraoperative conversation. *British Journal of Anaesthesia* 57:174–179.

Berger, H. 1929. Über das electrokephalogram des menschen, *Archiv Psychiatrie u. Nervenkrankheit* 87: 527–570.

Berns, G. S., J. D. Cohen, and M. A. Mintun. 1997. Brain regions responsive to novelty in the absence of awareness. *Science* 276: 1272–1275.

Bogen, J. E. 1986. One brain, two brains, or both? Two hemispheres—one brain: functions of corpus callosum. *Neurology & Neurobiology* 17:21–34.

———. 1995. On the neurophysiology of consciousness. I: An overview. *Consciousness & Cognition* 4(1):52–62.

Bonke, B., P. I. M. Schmitz, F. Verhage, and A. Zwaveling. 1986. A clinical study of so-called unconscious perception during general anaesthesia. *British Journal of Anaesthesia* 58:957–964.

Bower, B. 1999. *Science News* 156:280.

Buchner, H., M. Fuchs, H. A. Wischmann, O. Dossel, I. Ludwig, A. Knepper, and P. Berg. 1994. Source analysis of median nerve and finger stimulated somatosensory evoked potentials. *Brain Topography* 6(4): 299–310.

Buchner, H., R. Gobbelé, M. Wagner, M. Fuchs, T. D. Waberski, and R. Beckmann. 1997. Fast visual evoked potential input into human area V5. Neuroreport 8(11):2419–2422.

Burns, B. D. 1951. Some properties of isolated cerebral cortex in the unanesthetized cat. *Journal of Physiology (London)* 112:156–175.

———. 1954. The production of after-bursts in isolated unanesthetized cerebral cortex. *Journal of Physiology (London)* 125:427–446.

Burns, J. 1991. Does consciousness perform a function independently of the brain? *Frontier Perspectives* 2(1):19–34.

Buser, P. 1998. *Cerveau de soi, cerveau de l'autre* [One's brain and the brain of another]. Paris: Odile Jacob, see pp. 30–73.

Chalmers, D. J. 1995. Facing up to the problem of consciousness. *Journal of Consciousness Studies* 2(3):200–219.

———. 1996. *The Conscious Mind*. New York: Oxford University Press.

Churchland, P. M., and P. S. Churchland. 1998. *On the Contrary: Critical Essays, 1987–1997*. Cambridge, Mass.: MIT Press.

Churchland, P. S. 1981. On the alleged backwards referral of experiences and its relevance to the mind-body problem. *Philosophy of Science* 48:165–181.

Chusid, J. G., and J. J. MacDonald. 1958. *Correlative Neuro-anatomy and Functional Neurology.* Los Altos, Calif.: Lange Medical Publishers, p. 175.

Clark, R. E., and L. R. Squire, 1998. Classical conditioning and brain systems: the role of awareness. *Science* 280:77–81.

Cooper, D. A. 1997. *God Is a Verb: Kabbalah and the Practice of Mystical Judaism.* New York: Penguin Putnam.

Crawford, B. H. 1947. Visual adaptation in relation to brief conditioning stimuli. *Proceedings of the Royal Society Series B (London)* 134:283–302.

Crick, F. 1994. *The Astonishing Hypothesis.* London: Simon and Schuster.

Crick, F., and C. Koch. 1998. Consciousness and neuroscience. *Cerebral Cortex* 8(2):92–107.

Cushing, H. 1909. A note upon the faradic stimulation of the postcentral gyrus in conscious patients. *Brain* 32:44–53.

Damasio, A. R. 1994. *Descartes' Error.* New York: Penguin Putnam.

———. 1997. Neuropsychology. Towards a neuropathology of emotion and mood. *Nature* 386(6627):769–770.

———. 1999. *The Feeling of What Happens: Body and Emotions in the Making of Consciousness.* New York: Harcourt Brace.

Del Guidice, E. 1993. Coherence in condensed and living matter. *Frontier Perspectives* 3(2):6–20.

Dember, W. N., and D. G. Purcell. 1967. Recovery of masked visual targets by inhibition of the masking stimulus. *Science* 157:1335–1336.

Dennett, D. C. 1984. *Elbow Room: The Varieties of Free Will Worth Wanting.* Cambridge, Mass.: Bradford Books (MIT Press).

————. 1991. *Consciousness Explained.* Boston: Little, Brown and Company.

————. 1993. Discussion in Libet, B. The neural time factor in conscious and unconscious events. In: *Experimental and Theoretical Studies of Consciousness.* Ciba Foundation Symposium #174. Chichester, England: John Wiley and Sons.

Dennett, D. C., and M. Kinsbourne. 1992. Time and the observer: the where and when of consciousness in the brain. *Behavioral and Brain Sciences* 15:183–247.

Descartes, R. 1644 [1972]. *Treatise of Man,* trans. T. S. Hall. Cambridge, Mass.: Harvard University Press.

Doty, R. W. 1969. Electrical stimulation of the brain in behavioral cortex. *Annual Reviews of Physiology* 20:289–320.

————. 1984. Some thoughts and some experiments on memory. In *Neuropsychology of Memory,* eds. L. R. Squire and N. Butters. New York: Guilford.

————. 1998. Five mysteries of the mind, and their consequences. *Neuropsychologia* 36:1069–1076.

————. 1999. Two brains, one person. *Brain Research Bulletin* 50:46.

Drachman, D. A., and J. Arbit. 1966. Memory and the hippocampal complex: is memory a multiple process? *Archives of Neurology* 15(1):52–61.

Eccles, J. C. 1966. *Brain and Conscious Experience.* New York: Springer-Verlag.

————. 1990. A unitary hypothesis of mind-brain interaction in cerebral cortex. *Proceedings of the Royal Society B (London)* 240:433–451.

Echlin, F. A., V. Arnett, and J. Zoll. 1952. Paroxysmal high voltage discharges from isolated and partially isolated human and animal cerebral cortex. *Electroencephalography & Clinical Neurophysiology* 4:147–164.

Edelman, G. M., and V. B. Mountcastle, eds. 1978. *The Mindful Brain.* Cambridge, Mass.: MIT Press.

Feinstein, B., W. W. Alberts, E. W. Wright, Jr., and G. Levin. 1960. A stereotoxic technique in man allowing multiple spatial and temporal approaches to intracranial targets. *Journal of Neurosurgery* 117:708–720.

Feynman, R. 1990. In: *No Ordinary Genius,* ed. C. Sykes. New York: W. W. Norton, p. 252.

Franco, R. 1989. Intuitive science. *Nature* 338:536.

Freud, S. 1915 [1955]. *The Unconscious.* London: Hogarth Press.

Gazzaniga, M. S. 1998. Brain and conscious experience. *Advances in Neurology* 77:181–192, plus discussion on pp. 192–193.

Goff, G. A., Y. Matsumiya, T. Allison, and W. R. Goff. 1977. The scalp topography of human somatosensory and auditory evoked potentials. *Electroencephalography & Clinical Neurophysiology* 42:57–76.

Goldberg, G., and K. K. Bloom. 1990. The alien hand sign: localization, lateralization and recovery. *American Journal of Physical Medicine and Rehabilitation* 69:228–230.

Goldring, S., J. L. O'Leary, T. G. Holmes, and M. J. Jerva. 1961. Direct response of isolated cerebral cortex of cat. *Journal of Neurophysiology* 24:633–650.

Gray, C. M., and W. Singer. 1989. Stimulus-specific neuronal oscillations in orientation columns of cat visual cortex. *Proceedings of the National Academy of Sciences, U.S.A.* 86:1698–1702.

Green, D. M. and J. A. Swets. 1966. *Signal Detection Theory and Psychophysics.* New York: John Wiley and Sons.

Grossman, R. G. 1980. Are current concepts and methods in neuroscience adequate for studying the neural basis of consciousness and mental activity? In: *Information Processing in the Nervous System,* eds. H. H. Pinsker and W. D. Willis, Jr. New York: Raven Press, pp. 331–338.

Haggard, P., and M. Eimer. 1999. On the relation between brain potentials and conscious awareness. *Experimental Brain Research* 126:128–133.

Haggard, P., and B. Libet. 2001. Conscious intention and brain activity. *Journal of Consciousness Studies* 8:47–64.

Halliday, A. M., and R. Mingay. 1961. Retroactive raising of a sensory threshold by a contralateral stimulus. *Quarterly Journal of Experimental Psychology* 13:1–11.

Hawking, S. 1988. *A Brief History of Time.* New York: Bantam Books.

Hook, S., ed. 1960. *Dimensions of Mind.* Washington Square: New York University Press.

Hubel, D. H, and T. N. Wiesel. 1962. Receptive fields, binocular interaction and functional architecture in the cat's visual cortex. *Journal of Physiology (London)* 160:106–134.

Ingvar, D. H. 1955. Extraneuronal influences upon the electrical activity of isolated cortex following stimulation of the reticular activating system. *Acta Physiologica Scand* 33:169–193.

———. 1979. Hyperfrontal distribution of the cerebral grey matter blood flow in resting wakefulness: on the functional anatomy of the conscious state. *Acta Neurologica Scand.* 60:12–25.

———. 1999. On volition: a neuro-physiologically oriented essay. In *The Volitional Brain: Towards a Neuroscience of Free Will,* eds. B. Libet, A. Freeman, and K. Sutherland. Thorverton: Imprint Academic, pp. 1–10.

Ingvar, D., and L. Phillipson. 1977. Distribution of cerebral blood flow in the dominant hemisphere during motor ideation and motor performance. *Annals of Neurology* 2:230–237.

James, W. 1890. *The Principles of Psychology.* New York: Dover.

Japenga, A. 1999. Philosophy: the new therapy for 2000. *USA Weekend,* October 22–24.

Jasper, H., and G. Bertrand. 1966. Recording with micro-electrodes in stereotaxic surgery for Parkinson's disease. *Journal of Neurosurgery* 24:219–224.

Jeannerod, M. 1997. *The Cognitive Neuroscience of Action.* Oxford: Blackwell.

Jensen, A. R. 1979. "g": outmoded theory of unconquered frontier. *Creative Science and Technology* 2:16–29.

Josephson, B. D. 1993. Report on a symposium on reductionism in science and culture. *Frontier Perspectives* 3(2):29–32.

Jung, R., A. Hufschmidt, and W. Moschallski. 1982. Slow brain potentials in writing: The correlation between writing hand and speech dominance in right-handed humans. *Archiv fur Pschiatrie und Nervenkrankheiten* 232:305–324.

Kaufmann, W. 1961. *Faith of a Heretic.* New York: Doubleday.

Keller, I., and H. Heckhausen. 1990. Readiness potentials preceding spontaneous acts: voluntary vs. involuntary control. *Electroencephalography and Clinical Neurophysiology* 76:351–361.

Kihlstrom, J. F. 1984. Conscious, subconscious, unconscious: a cognitive perspective. In: *The Unconscious Reconsidered,* eds. K. S. Bowers and D. Meichenbaum. New York: John Wiley and Sons.

———. 1993. The psychological unconscious and the self. In: *Experimental and Theoretical Studies of Consciousness.* Ciba Foundation Symposium #174. Chichester, England: John Wiley and Sons.

———. 1996. Perception without awareness of what is perceived, learning without awareness of what is learned. In: *The Science of Consciousness:*

*Psychological, Neuropsychological, and Clinical Reviews,* ed. M. Velmans. London: Routledge.

Koestler, A. 1964. *The Art of Creation.* London: Picador Press.

Kornbuber, H. H., and L. Deecke. 1965. Hirnpotential ändrungen bei Willkürbewegungen und passiven Bewegungen des Menschen: Bereitschaftpotential und reafferente potentiale. *Pflügers Archiv* 284:1–17.

Kristiansen, K., and G. Courtois. 1949. Rhythmic electrical activity from isolated cerebral cortex. *Electroencephalography and Clinical Neurophysiology* 1:265–272.

Laplace, P. S. 1914 [1951]. *A Philosophical Essay on Probabilities,* trans. F. W. Truscott and F. I. Emory. New York: Dover.

Lassen, N. A., and D. H. Ingvar. 1961. The blood flow of the cerebral cortex determined by radioactive Krypton 85. *Experientia* 17:42–43.

Libet, B. 1965. Cortical activation in conscious and unconscious experience. *Perspectives in Biology and Medicine* 9:77–86.

———. 1966. Brain stimulation and the threshold of conscious experience. In *Brain and Conscious Experience,* ed. J. C. Eccles. New York: Springer-Verlag, pp. 165–181.

———. 1973. Electrical stimulation of cortex in human subjects and conscious sensory aspects, In *Handbook of Sensory Physiology,* ed. A. Iggo. Berlin: Springer-Verlag, pp. 743–790.

———. 1980. Commentary on J. R. Searle's "Mind, Brains and Programs." *Behavioral and Brain Sciences* 3:434.

———. 1985. Unconscious cerebral initiative and the role of conscious will in voluntary action. *Behavioral and Brain Sciences* 8:529–566.

———. 1987. Consciousness: conscious, subjective experience. In: *Encyclopedia of Neuroscience,* ed. G. Adelman. Boston: Birkhäuser, pp. 271–275.

————. 1989. Conscious subjective experience and unconscious mental functions: a theory of the cerebral processes involved. In: *Models of Brain Function*, ed. R. M. J. Cotterill. Cambridge, England: Cambridge University Press, pp. 35–49.

————. 1993a. *Neurophysiology of Consciousness: Selected Papers and New Essays by Benjamin Libet*. Boston: Birkhäuser.

————. 1993b. The neural time factor in conscious and unconscious events. In: *Experimental and Theoretical Studies of Consciousness*. Ciba Foundation Symposium #174. Chichester, England: John Wiley and Sons, pp. 123–146.

————. 1994. A testable field theory of mind-brain interaction. *Journal of Consciousness Studies* 1(1):119–126.

————. 1996. Solutions to the hard problem of consciousness. *Journal of Consciousness Studies* 3:33–35.

————. 1997. Conscious mind as a force field: a reply to Lindhal & Århem. *Journal of Theoretical Biology* 185:137–138.

————. 1999. Do we have free will? *Journal of Consciousness Studies* 6(8–9):47–57.

————. 2001. "Consciousness, free action and the brain": commentary on John Searle's article. *Journal of Consciousness Studies* 8(8):59–65.

————. 2003. Timing of conscious experience: reply to the 2002 commentaries on Libet's findings. *Consciousness and Cognition* 12: 321–331.

Libet, B., W. W. Alberts, E. W. Wright, L. Delattre, G. Levin, and B. Feinstein. 1964. Production of threshold levels of conscious sensation by electrical stimulation of human somatosensory cortex. *Journal of Neurophysiology* 27:546–578.

Libet, B., W. W. Alberts, E. W. Wright, and B. Feinstein. 1967. Responses of human somatosensory cortex to stimuli below threshold for conscious sensation. *Science* 158:1597–1600.

Libet, B., D. K. Pearl, D. E. Morledge, C. A. Gleason, Y. Hosobuchi, and N. M. Barbaro. 1991. Control of the transition from sensory detection to sensory awareness in man by the duration of a thalamic stimulus: the cerebral "time-on" factor. *Brain* 114:1731–1757.

Libet, B., C. A. Gleason, E. W. Wright, and D. K. Pearl. 1983. Time of conscious intention to act in relation to onset of cerebral activities (readiness-potential): the unconscious initiation of a freely voluntary act. *Brain* 106:623–642.

Libet, B., E. W. Wright, Jr., B. Feinstein, and D. K. Pearl. 1979. Subjective referral of the timing for a conscious sensory experience: a functional role for the somatosensory specific projection system in man. *Brain* 102:193–224.

———. 1992. Retroactive enhancement of a skin sensation by a delayed cortical stimulus in man: evidence for delay of a conscious sensory experience. *Consciousness and Cognition* 1:367–375.

Libet, B., E. W. Wright, and C. Gleason. 1982. Readiness-potentials preceding unrestricted "spontaneous" vs. pre-planned voluntary acts. *Electroencephalography & Clinical Neurophysiology* 54:322–335.

Marshall, J. C. 1989. An open mind? *Nature* 339:25–26.

Marshall, L. H., and H. W. Magoun. 1998. *Discoveries in the Human Brain.* Totowa, N.J.: Humana Press.

McGinn, C. 1997. *Minds and Bodies: Philosophers and Their Ideas.* London: Oxford University Press.

———. 1999. Can we ever understand consciousness? *The New York Review,* June 10, 1999, pp. 44–48.

Melchner, L. von, S. L. Pallas, and M. Sur. 2000. Visual behavior mediated by retinal projections directed to the auditory pathway. *Nature* 404:871–876.

Mountcastle, V. B. 1957. Modalities and topographic properties of single neurons in sensory cortex. *Journal of Neurophysiology* 20:408–434.

Mukhopadhyary, A.K. 1995. *Conquering the Brain.* New Delhi: Conscious Publications.

Nichols, M. J., and W. T. Newsome. 1999. Monkeys play the odds. *Nature* 400:217–218.

Nishimura, H. 1999. Visual stimuli activate auditory cortex in the deaf. *Cortex* 9:392–405.

Palm, A. 1991. Book review of *The Emperor's New Mind* by R. Penrose. *Frontier Perspectives* 2(1):27–28.

Penfield, W. 1958. *The Excitable Cortex in Conscious Man.* Liverpool: Liverpool University Press.

Penfield, W., and E. Boldrey. 1937. Somatic, motor and sensory representation in the cerebral cortex of man as studied by electrical stimulation. *Brain* 60:389–443.

Penfield, W., and H. Jasper. 1954. *Epilepsy and the Functional Anatomy of the Human Brain.* Boston: Little, Brown and Company.

Penfield, W., and T. B. Rasmussen. 1950. *The Cerebral Cortex of Man.* New York: Macmillan Books.

Penrose, R. 1989. *The Emperor's New Mind: Concerning Computers, Minds and the Laws of Physics.* London: Oxford University Press.

Pepper, S. C. 1960. A neural-identity theory of mind. In: *Dimensions of Mind,* ed. S. Hook. Washington Square: New York University Press, pp. 37–55.

Pieron, H., and J. Segal. 1939. Sur un phenomene de facilitation retroactive dan l'excitation electrique de branches nerveuses cutanées sensibilité tactile. *Journal of Neurophysiology* 2:178–191.

Pippard, B. 1992. Counsel of despair: review of *Understanding the Present Science and the Soul of Modern Man, Doubleday. Nature* 357:29.

Poincaré, H. 1913. *Foundations of Science.* New York: Science Press.

Poppel, E. 1988. *Time and Conscious Experience.* New York: Harcourt Brace Jovanovich.

Popper, K. R. 1953. Language and the body-mind problem: a restatement of interactivism. In: *Proceedings of the XIth International Congress of Philosophy,* vol. 7. Amsterdam: North Holland Press, pp. 101–107.

———. 1992. *In Search of a Better World: Lectures and Essays from Thirty Years.* London: Routledge.

Popper, K. R., and J. C. Eccles. 1977. *The Self and Its Brain.* Heidelberg: Springer-Verlag.

Popper, K. R., B. I. B. Lindahl, and P. Århem. 1993. A discussion of the mind-body problem. *Theoretical Medicine* 14:167–180.

Ray, P. G., K. J. Meador, C. M. Epstein, D. W. Loring, and L. J. Day. 1998. Magnetic stimulation of visual cortex: factors influencing the perception of phosphenes. *Journal of Clinical Neurophysiology* 15(4):351–357.

Ray, P. G., K. J. Meador, J. R. Smith, J. W. Wheless, M. Sittenfeld, and G. L. Clifton. 1999. Physiology of perception: cortical stimulation and recording in humans. *Neurology* 52(2):1044–1049.

Roland, P. E., and L. Freiberg. 1985. Localization of cortical areas activated by thinking. *Journal of Neurophysiology* 53:1219–1243.

Rosenthal, D. M. 2002. The timing of conscious states. *Consciousness & Cognition* 11(2):215–220.

Schreiber, F. R. 1973 [1974]. *Sybil,* 2nd ed. New York: Regnery Warner Books.

Schwartz, J., and S. Begley. 2002. *The Mind and the Brain: Neuroplasticity and the Power of Mental Force.* New York: Regan Books.

Searle, J. R. 1980. Minds, brains and programs. *Behavioral and Brain Sciences* 3(3):417–457.

————. 1992. *The Rediscovery of the Mind*. Cambridge, Mass.: MIT Press.

————. 1993. Discussion in Libet, B. The neural time factor in conscious and unconscious events. In: *Experimental and Theoretical Studies of Consciousness*. Ciba Foundation Symposium #174. Chichester, England: John Wiley and Sons, p. 156.

————. 2000a. Consciousness, free action and the brain. *Journal of Consciousness Studies* 7(10):3–32.

————. 2000b. Consciousness. *Annual Review of Neuroscience 2000* 23:557–578.

Sharma, J., A. Angelucci, and M. Sur. 2000. Visual behavior mediated by retinal projections directed to the auditory pathway. *Nature* 404:841–847.

Sherrington, C.S. 1940. *Man on His Nature*. Cambridge, England: Cambridge University Press.

Shevrin, H. 1973. Brain wave correlates of subliminal stimulation, unconscious attention, primary- and secondary-process thinking, and repressiveness. *Psychological Issues* 8(2); Monograph 30:56–87.

Shevrin, H., and S. Dickman. 1980. The psychological unconscious: a necessary assumption for all psychological theory? *American Psychologist* 35:421–434.

Singer, I. B. 1968 [1981]. Interview by H. Flender. In: *Writers at Work,* ed. G. Plimpton. New York: Penguin Books.

Singer, W. 1990. Search for coherence: a basic principle of cortical self-organization. *Concepts in Neuroscience* 1:1–26.

————. 1991. Response synchronization of cortical neurons: an epiphenomenon of a solution to the binding problem. *IBRO News* 19:6–7.

————. 1993. Synchronization of cortical activity and its putative role in information processing and learning. *Annual Review of Physiology* 55:349–374.

Snyder, F. W., and N. H. Pronko. 1952. *Vision and Spatial Inversion*. Wichita, Kans.: University of Wichita.

Sokoloff, L., M. Reivich, C. Kennedy, M. H. Des Rosiers, C. S. Patlake, K. D. Petttigrew, D. Sakurada, and M. Shinohara. 1977. The [$^{14}$C] deoxyglucose method for the measurement of local cerebral glucose utilization; theory, procedure, and normal values in the conscious and anesthetized albino rat. *Journal of Neurochemistry* 28:897–916.

Spence, S. A. 1996. Free will in the light of neuro-psychiatry. *Philosophy, Psychiatry & Psychology* 3:75–90.

Sperry, R. W. 1947. Cerebral regulation of motor coordination in monkeys following multiple transection of sensorimotor cortex. *Journal of Neurophysiology* 10:275–294.

————. 1950. Neural basis of spontaneous optokinetic response produced by visual inversion. *Journal of Comparative and Physiological Psychology* 43:482–489.

————. 1952. Neurology and the mind-brain problem. *American Scientist* 40:291–312.

————. 1980. Mind-brain interaction: mentalism, yes; dualism, no. *Neuroscience* 5:195–206.

————. 1984. Consciousness, personal identity and the divided brain. *Neuropsychologia* 22:661–673.

————. 1985. *Science and Moral Priority*. Westport: Praeger.

Sperry, R. W., M. S Gazzaniga, and J. E. Bogen. 1969. Interhemispheric relationships: the neocortical commissures. Syndromes of hemisphere disconnection. In: *Handbook of Clinical Neurology*, eds. P. J. Vinken and G. W. Bruyn. Amsterdam: North Holland Press, pp. 273–290.

Spiegel, H. 1997. Interview by M. Borch-Jacobsen, "Sybil—The Making of a Disease," *The New York Review,* April 24, 1997, pp. 60–64.

Stoerig, P. and A. Cowey. 1995. Blindsight in monkeys. *Nature* 373:147–249.

Stoerig, P., A. Zantanon, and A. Cowey. 2002. Aware or unaware: assessment of critical blindness in four men and a monkey. *Cerebral Cortex* 12(6):565–574.

Stratton, G. M. 1897. Vision without inversion of the retinal image. *Psychological Review* 4:341–360.

Taylor, J. L., and D. I. McCloskey. 1990. Triggering of pre-programmed movements as reactions to masked stimuli. *Journal of Neurophysiology* 63:439–446.

Vallbö, A.B., K. A. Olsson, K. G. Westberg and F. J. Clark. 1984. Microstimulation of single tactile afferents from the human hand. *Brain* 107:727–749.

Velmans, M. 1991. Is human information processing conscious? *Behavioral and Brain Sciences* 14:651–669.

———. 1993. Discussion in *Experimental and Theoretical Studies of Consciousness,* Ciba Foundation Symposium #174, Chichester, England: John Wiley and Sons, pp. 145–146.

Wegner, D. M. 2002. *The Illusion of Conscious Will.* Cambridge, Mass.: Bradford Books (MIT Press).

Weiskrantz, L. 1986. *Blindsight: A Case Study and Implications.* Oxford: Clarendon Press.

Whitehead, A. N. 1911. Quoted by Bruce Bower. 1999. *Science News* 156:280.

———. 1925. *Science and the Modern World.* New York: McMillan.

Wieseltier, L. 1987. Book review of *More Die of Heartbreak* by S. Bellow. *The New Republic,* August 31, 1987, pp. 36–38.

Wittgenstein, L. 1953. *Philosophical Investigations*. Oxford: Basil Blackwell.

Wolf, S. S., D. W. Jones, M. B. Knable, J. G. Gorey, K. S. Lee, T. M. Hyde, R. S. Coppola, and D. R. Weinberger. 1996. Tourette syndrome: prediction of phenotypic variation in monozygotic twins by caudate nucleus $D_2$ receptor binding. *Science* 273:1225–1227.

Wood, C. C., D. D. Spencer, T. Allison, G. McCarthy, P. P. Williamson, and W. R. Goff. 1988. Localization of human somatosensory cortex during surgery by cortical surface recording of somatosensory evoked potential. *Journal of Neurosurgery* 68(1):99–111.

Wouk, H. 1988. *This Is My God*. Boston: Little, Brown and Company.

Damasio, A. R., 94, 187, 188, 204
daydreaming, 96–99
DCRs, direct cortical responses, 19, 40, 58
Death, 6, 8, 31, 214, 216, 219, 220
Deecke, L., 124, 130
delayed conditioning, 51
delay in sensory awareness, 33, 45, 46, 50, 51, 55, 70, 71, 73, 75, 77, 86, 91, 199; half-second delay, 46, 50, 68, 70, 72, 75, 80, 88, 112, 123, 132, 199
deliberation, 132, 135, 148, 149, 155
Dennett, Daniel, 18, 59, 64–66, 152, 159
Descartes, R., 10, 79, 160, 181, 185, 186, 187, 188, 193, 198
Descartes, "thinking," 186, 187, 188
Descartes, not thinking, 188
determinism and free will, 6, 151, 154, 156, 168, 198, 215, 216; as illusion, 144, 152; non-determinism, 152–154; scientific options, 156
determinist materialism, 5, 6
Dickman, S., 94, 207
discontinuity of conscious events, 112
Doctorow, E. L., 108
Doty, Robert W., 133, 134, 139, 156, 162, 165, 168, 171, 210
dreaming, 14, 92, 96, 97
dualism, 86, 181, 182, 183, 186, 194

Eccles, Sir John, 12, 125, 165, 167, 168, 179, 204, 216
Echlin, F. A., 174, 176
Eddington, Sir Arthur, 162
Edelman, G. M., 166
Eimer, M., 135

Einstein, Albert, 6, 7, 183
electrical stimulation, 18, 26, 35, 37; conscious responses to, 45, 177; for intractable pain, 31; repetitive stimulus pulses, 45; of sensory cortex, 18, 177, 178; of "silent" areas, 27; of skin, 35, 51; stimulus intensities, 39, 41, 42, 49, 56–58, 66, 73, 103, 116; subliminal pulses, 56, 106, 118; of temporal lobe, 177; train durations of pulses, 39, 40, 45, 49, 57, 58; of visual and auditory cortex, 177
electroconvulsive shock therapy, 54, 65
electrophysiology, 23
emergent phemonema, 162, 163, 203
emergent property, 86, 169
endogenous conscious electroencephalogram (EEG), 24, 25, 176, 217; brain functions, 89, 113, 128, 147; "brain waves," 24, 217
ethical implications, 140, 149, 151, 191, 197; guilt, 150, 151, 201, 202, 208; self-control, 20, 149
event-related-potentials (ERPs), 47, 48; later components of, 48, 74, 77
evoked potentials (EPs), 47, 69, 70, 77, 85, 113
existentialist view, 72
eyelid blink reflex, 93

fate, 140, 141
Feinstein, Bertram, 28, 29, 30, 31, 34
ferrets, 84
Feynman, Richard, 9
Foerster, O., 108
forced choice, 15, 111, 116, 117, 119

Forster, E. M., 108
Franco, R., 96
freely voluntary act, 2, 123, 126, 129, 139, 141, 142, 147, 151; definition of, 128, 129; initiation by brain, 123; unconscious initiation, 142, 144
free will, 4, 123, 125, 133, 136, 139, 141, 143, 144, 145, 146, 149, 151, 152, 154–156, 161, 166, 167, 197, 198, 201, 212, 215, 222; control function, 146, 222; do we have it?, 123, 140; Kabbalist view, 141; trigger function, 142, 145, 197; unconscious acts, 140; unconscious initiation, 140, 145
Freud, S., 2, 71, 120, 122, 200
Friberg, L., 22, 179
functionalism, 11

Gerard, R. W., 29
"ghost in machine," 183, 221
Goff, W. R., 69
Golden Rules, 150
Goldring, S. J., 174
Granit, Ragnar, 12
Gray, C. M., 166
Grossman, R., 42
guessing responses, 104, 105, 106, 117

Haggard, P., 135
Halliday, A. M., 51
Hawking, S., 183
Heckhausen, H., 135
hippocampus, 26, 60, 61, 62, 63, 64; bilateral loss of, 61, 62
Houdini, H., 220
human subjects, 9, 15, 22, 27, 60, 117, 129, 176, 177, 222

hunch, 94
hypnosis, age regression under, 209

identical twins, 211
identity theory, 12, 13, 87, 146, 158, 159, 182
imagination of moving, 179
informed consent, 29, 30, 177
Ingvar, David, 21, 22, 172, 174
initiating an act, experience of, 23, 93, 123, 124, 136, 137, 139, 144, 149, 161, 197, 202, 222
inner quality, 12, 87, 159
intention to act, 98, 109, 113, 123, 126, 142; awareness of, 98, 109, 123, 147
introspective reports, 8, 9, 10, 11, 13, 16, 18, 29, 59, 85, 158, 169, 178; and behaviorism, 11, 17; non-verbal, 10; as objective evidence, 11; reliability of, 10
intuitive feeling, 94, 155
involuntary acts, 129, 142
isolated slab of cortex, 173–177; awake condition and, 176–177; properties of, 176–177; Sperry technique, 174–175

James, William, 1, 112
Japenga, Ann, 220
Jasper, Herbert, 12, 18, 19, 48
Jensen, Arthur, 54, 55
Josephson, Brian D., 162, 216
Jung, R., 108

Keller, I., 135
Kihlstrom, J. R., 94, 100
Koch, Christof, 4
Koestler, A., 97
Kornhuber, H. H., 124, 130
Kristiansen, K., 174

Laplace, P. S., 17
Lassen, N. A., 21
lateral RPs (LRP), 135
Leibniz, N., 153
Leksell stereotaxic frame, 28
lesions in brain, 15, 19, 20, 30, 63, 204, 205, 206, 207
Libet, B., 30, 38, 40, 48, 49, 50, 52, 56, 58, 59, 64, 65, 66, 67, 73, 77, 85, 98, 102, 113, 126, 127, 131, 135, 137, 145, 147, 155, 158, 161, 166, 168, 169, 170, 177, 201, 202, 213
Libet, Fay, 98
Loewi, O., 96, 97
Lundberg, Anders, 12

magnetic resonance imaging (MRI), 22, 23, 179; neural changes in time, 23; resolution of time, 23
magnetoencephalogram (MEG), 25
maps of cortex, 36
Marshall, John C., 31
Marshall, L. and H. W. Magoun, 4
materialism, eliminative, 5, 6, 159
McGinn, Colin, 159, 160, 183
Meador, K., 42, 43
medial lemniscus, 43, 44, 45, 56, 75, 76, 78, 147
medulla oblongata, 43
Melchner, L. von, 84
memory, 15, 26, 54, 59, 60, 61, 62, 64, 65, 66, 94, 180, 205, 209, 218; explicit (declarative), 60, 61, 64; implicit (nondeclarative), 61, 62; role in awareness, 59, 60, 63, 64, 66, 92
mental events, discontinuous, 114
mental influence, neuronal, 166, 167,

178; dualistic solution, 167, 181, 183; monistic solutions, 167
mental telepathy, 171
mental unity, 191
mind, as loose cannon, 183, 184
mind, not divisible, 181, 190, 193
mind and brain, separation of, 192, 194
mind-brain relation, 7, 16, 85, 86, 125, 146, 160, 161, 164, 166, 168, 180, 216, 222
Mingay, R., 51
models or theories, 3, 17, 136, 161, 203
motor units, 114, 115
Mountcastle, V., 164, 166
Mt. Zion Hospital, San Francisco, 30
Mukhopadhyay, A. K., 181
multiple personality disorder (MPD), 205, 208

Nagel, Thomas, 12
near-death experiences, 216, 217, 218, 219; experimental tests of, 219, 220
neuronal representations, 165
neuronal time, 72, 122
Newsome, W. T., 94
Newton, 17
Nichols, M. J., 94

objective scientific study, 186
obsessive-compulsive disorder (OCD), 142, 143
outer quality, 87, 159
overlapping events, 114

Palm, Ann, 212
paradoxical timings, 75
Penfield, Wilder, 129, 177

Penrose, R., 212
Pepper, Stephen, 12, 87
perceptions of reality, 72
personal identity, 4, 204, 205, 206, 210;
    amnesia and, 205; and cerebral hemi-
    sphere loss, 205; "split brain," 210
Phillips, Charles, 12
Phillipson, L., 179
Phineas Gage, 20
physical vs. non-physical activities, 3,
    158, 160, 161, 168, 221
physical vs. subjective, 2, 3, 5, 9, 14, 27,
    32, 153, 157, 158, 159, 162, 163, 168, 169,
    179, 183, 184, 221, 222; unexplained
    gap between, 153; and violation of
    laws, 154
pineal gland, 181, 190, 191
Pippard, Sir Brian, 216
pitched ball, timings, 110
playing musical instruments, 97, 109,
    200
Poincaré, H., 95, 96, 195
Poppel, E., 198
Popper, Karl, 3, 6, 12, 125, 152, 165, 169,
    189, 190, 204, 212, 216
positron emission tomography (PET),
    22, 23, 179
postcentral gyrus, 26, 40, 44, 83, 177
postsynaptic responses, 24
preceding voluntary act, 131, 141
precentral gyrus, 26
preplanning, 129, 130, 131, 132, 133, 136,
    137, 148, 149, 155
preset timing, 129
primary EP, 47, 48, 49, 50, 67, 74, 75, 76,
    78, 80, 85, 86; function of, 67; sensa-
tion, 47; scalp recording, 70, 124; tim-
    ing signal, 76, 86
primary sensory cortex, 18, 84, 85
professional sports, 110, 136

qualia, 14

Rasmussen, T. B., 37, 129
Ray, P. G., 42
reaction times (RT), 54, 55, 111, 136, 199;
    deliberate lengthening of, 55
readiness potential (RP), 108, 124, 125,
    126, 127, 129, 130, 131, 132, 133, 134, 135,
    136, 137, 138, 139, 141, 142, 148, 149
reductionism, 215, 216
regional cerebral blood flow (rCBF), 21,
    22; in motor activity, 21; in thought
    processes, 21
responsibility, 140, 202, 208, 210
retinal pathway, 84
retroactive enhancement, 52, 54, 65
right hemisphere, 37, 67, 170, 171, 210;
    conscious?, 171
Roland, P. E., 179
Rolandic fissure, 26, 36, 37, 44
Rosenthal, David M., 201, 202, 203
RPI, 132, 133, 134, 135
RPII, 132, 133, 134, 135, 136, 149
Russell, Bertrand, 108

Schreiber, Flora R., 209
Schwartz, J. M., 143, 220
Searle, John, 99, 100, 135, 136, 159, 160,
    161, 212
self, 1, 8, 13, 136, 161, 171, 203, 204, 205,
    206, 207, 208, 209, 210, 211, 212, 213,

214, 215, 216; autobiographical, 204,
    205, 206; awareness of, 4, 13, 86;
    "core self," 204; resistance to change,
    204; transient self, 204
self, singular, 208
self and soul, 6, 7, 191, 192, 194, 203,
    204, 211, 213, 214, 215, 216, 220, 221
self-awareness, 13, 86
self-initiated acts, 131, 137
self-paced acts, 130
selves one or two, 171, 211
sensory awareness delayed. *See* delay in
    sensory awareness
sensory modality vs. cortical area, 68,
    164
sensory pathways, 48, 51, 68
sensory perception, at brain, 116, 117
Sharma, J., 84
Sherrington, Sir Charles, 165
Shevrin, H., 12, 94, 118, 120, 207
signal detection, 111, 116
silent cortex, 27
silicon chip brain, 213
sin, 150, 152
Singer, Isaac Bashevis, 156, 166
Singer, W., 166
singing, 109
single-case studies, 31
single skin pulse, 46, 50; delay for
    awareness, 46, 53–55
Sokoloff, Louis, 22
soul, 6, 7, 191, 192, 194, 203, 204, 211, 213,
    214, 215, 216, 220, 221
speaking, 108, 148, 171, 210
specific projection pathway, 45, 47, 81
speculations, 3, 113, 166, 204

Sperry, R. W., 12, 82, 87, 156, 162, 165,
    167, 168, 169, 170, 171, 174, 175, 210, 216
Spiegel, Herbert, 209
spinal cord, 7, 8, 35, 43, 44, 45, 92, 97, 217
Spinoza, B., 159, 215
split-brain patients, 171, 205, 210
Squire, L. R., 62, 63, 93
Stoerig, Petra, 15
stream of consciousness, 112, 114, 200
subjective experience, 2, 3, 7, 8–12, 14,
    16–18, 27–29, 32, 82, 84, 85, 87, 88,
    100, 121, 137, 153, 157–159, 162–164, 166,
    168, 169, 172, 180, 183, 184, 198, 200,
    201, 216, 218, 221, 222; accessible to
    individual only, 1, 8, 87, 91, 158, 163,
    169, 182, 183; arising from physical,
    157, 159, 163, 168; fundamental prop-
    erty, 163
subjective inner life, 1, 2, 221
subjective referral, 75, 77, 79, 81, 84, 222;
    as neural corrector, 81; mental
    sphere?, 186; neuronal mechanism,
    85
subjective referral of sensations, 80, 84,
    86; antedating, 68, 72, 75, 77, 78, 88,
    91, 98, 113, 132, 199, 200; retroactive
    referral in time, 78, 87, 88, 113, 121,
    199; spatial, 80, 87; temporal, 80, 87
subjective timing, 64, 67, 69, 72, 73, 76,
    78, 79, 81, 85, 113, 137
subliminal perception, 106, 118
subthreshold sensory responses, 38, 73
supplementary motor area (SMA), 37,
    132, 178
switching tasks, 133
Sybil story, 209

synaptic transmitter, 23, 24, 83, 96, 167, 176

synchronicity of sensations, 68, 69, 70, 78

Tasker, 42

testable hypotheses, 3, 17, 32, 55, 102, 136, 159, 161, 168, 172, 182

thalamus, 14, 19, 43, 44, 45, 49, 69, 103, 207; ventrobasal, 43

Thompson, Richard, 93

thought processes, 21, 95, 112

threshold sensory experience, 38, 73; liminal intensity of stimulus, 39, 40, 41, 42, 56, 57, 58, 73

timelessness, 88

"time-on," filter function, 115

"time-on," test, 102–106, 116, 118

time-on theory, 92, 101, 102, 103, 106, 107, 108, 109, 111, 112, 115, 116, 118, 120, 198, 199

timing "clock," 126, 127, 128, 130, 131, 132, 133, 134

timing of skin stimulus, 128, 131, 132, 133, 137

Tourette's syndrome, 129, 142, 143, 146

Turing paradigm, 212, 213

unconscious detection, 16, 101, 103, 106, 116, 117, 118; little delay, 106, 107, 117; reaction time (RT), 54, 111, 136, 199

unconscious initiates conscious, 23, 89, 108, 124, 131, 136, 137, 144, 145, 147, 149, 150, 155, 161, 179, 197, 200, 201, 208

unconscious mental functions, 2, 7, 16, 32, 34, 71, 89, 90, 91, 92, 95, 96, 97, 98, 99, 100, 101, 102, 106, 111, 119, 144, 145, 146, 147, 148, 149, 196, 197, 198, 200, 201, 207, 208; distinction from conscious, 2, 8, 16, 38, 90, 91, 101, 102, 106, 117, 118, 119, 122, 144, 199, 222

unconscious solutions, 95, 96, 97, 98, 99

Velmans, Max, 66, 92, 145

visual image, subjective referral, 80

visual image upside down, 37, 45, 82

visuomotor referral, 82

voluntary acts, 93, 123, 125, 129, 131, 139, 141, 144, 148, 149, 151, 202

Wegner, D., 144, 152, 156

Weiskrantz, L., 117, 196

Whitehead, A. N., 95, 98

Wieseltier, L., 214, 215

Wigner, Eugene, 6, 157

Wilbur, Cornelia, 209

Wittgenstein, Ludwig, 88

writing, 97, 98, 109

yourself, 4, 140, 196, 198